# The C Primer

Les Hancock

Morris Krieger

## McGraw-Hill Book Company

New York   St. Louis   San Francisco   Auckland
Bogotá   Hamburg   Johannesburg London
Madrid   Mexico   Montreal   New Delhi
Panama   Paris   São Paulo   Singapore
Sydney   Tokyo   Toronto

1. C (Computer program language) I. Krieger, Morris,
date.   II. Title.
QA76.73.C15H36   1983   001.64'24   82-22897
ISBN 0-07-025981-X

   34567890   KGP/KGP   89876543

ISBN 0-07-025981-X

*This book was set in Times Roman and Monospace by the authors,*
*using a Graphic Systems Phototypesetter driven by*
*a PDP-11/45 running under the UNIX operating system.*

*Printed and bound by The Kingsport Press.*

# Table of Contents

# Introduction

A primer is a book for beginners. This primer is intended for those programmers who, while they may know something about programming, know nothing whatever about the C language; and the amount of programming knowledge we do assume our readers have is minimal. We assume they have access to a computer that runs C, and that they know enough about programming to create source code files using a system editor and then compile and run those files.

We don't pretend this primer contains a complete description of the C language. The appendix lists the features of C we don't describe. Nor will we be discussing any topic that requires a deep knowledge of systems programming, which happens to be the kind of programming C is particularly intended for. The discussion of such concepts would certainly have made the book a hard chew for our intended readers. More importantly, it would have obscured the clean, stripped-to-essentials outline of C a beginner needs and should have.

Perhaps our most important omission is that we say nothing about file handling. Most programs, whatever language they're written in, read data from files and write data to files. As almost everyone knows, C was meant to run under the UNIX® operating system, which has an excellent set of file-handling facilities. But we say nothing about UNIX or any of the other operating systems on which C may now be run. Therefore, as you make your way through our primer, or after you've finished it, you will have to consult the user's manual that is supplied with your operating system and follow the procedures described there to discover how to read from and write to files on your machine.

---

®Bell Telephone Laboratories

While C is a clean, straightforward language, and this is particularly so at the beginner's level at which this primer is written, there are two things about C that a beginner with some knowledge of another high-level language may find bothersome.  One has to do with C's relaxed attitude toward data typing; that is, the when, where, and how of declaring variables.  In contrast to Pascal, for example, which insists that variables be declared before they can be used, and always used as declared, C does not invariably insist that variables be declared in advance.  Instead, C has a system of automatic defaults.  If a programmer neglects to declare a variable before using it, at its first use in a program C will assume the programmer meant the variable to be of whatever type seems to be sensible to the compiler under the circumstances.  These default assumptions may not be what the programmer intended, and the result will be a great gnashing of teeth.  To avoid confusion, the beginner needn't take advantage of C's relaxed attitude toward data typing if he doesn't want to.  In fact, it would be better for him not to do so.  Instead, he should explicitly declare all his variables.

Another source of potential difficulty for the beginner has to do with C's pointer notation.  Pointers work by indirection, which is inherently a source of confusion.  Experienced assembly language programmers will readily grasp what C pointers are and what they are meant to do.  Others may not.  The simplest solution for those who are not familiar with pointers and find them confusing is simply not to use them.  In this case, their C programs will look and run much like the programs they might have written in one of the other structured languages.  Hopefully, they will in time discover how useful C pointers can be.

During the planning of this primer, it became apparent to us that a set of exercises would be extremely useful to a beginner, but we put off preparing them.  After we had completed the text, we discovered that someone had already written the exercises we had in mind.  The exercises are published in the form of a series of puzzles under the title, *The C Puzzle Book*, by Alan R. Feuer.*  We strongly urge our readers to obtain a copy of Feuer's book and work the appropriate puzzles as they complete the chapters in our primer.  The fit between the two books is not perfect, but it is very good.  In addition, Feuer touches on aspects of C we thought too advanced for a primer (e.g., casts, bitwise operators), but our readers should not find these topics difficult to understand.

Having completed this primer (and Feuer's puzzles), what can the

---

* Feuer, Alan R., *The C Puzzle Book.* Prentice-Hall, 1982.

interested beginner do next to consolidate and extend his knowledge of the C language? The answer is obvious: read *The C Programming Language*, by Kernighan and Ritchie.* Indeed, one of the objects of this primer is to bring the beginner up to the level where he can get more out of their book than he might otherwise for, truth to tell, *The C Programming Language* is not a book for beginning C programmers. It was in fact written to introduce C to experienced systems programmers for whom the underlying language and programming concepts were largely self-evident. The graceful clarity with which the book is written has in a sense proven deceptive, for it has made many beginners believe they could get through the book without too much trouble. Alas, they have instead found themselves hopelessly bogged down somewhere in Chapter 3. A warning to beginners is therefore still in order. Having completed this primer, they should find *The C Programming Language* much more accessible, but if they are unfamiliar with systems programming concepts there will still be much in Kernighan and Ritchie they will find difficult.

Another thing a beginner might do to learn what the programming art is all about is try working his way through the programs contained in *Software Tools*, by Kernighan and Plauger,† one of the best expositions on the art that has ever been written. We would recommend the original version of *Software Tools*, where the programs are written in Ratfor, for Ratfor and C are quite similar.

And, of course, the beginner should start writing his own programs in C as soon as possible. It is the only way to really learn the language.

## Acknowledgements

First, we want to thank Ed Yourdon for allowing us to use the computing facilities of Yourdon, Inc. for the preparation of the text. This entire book was written and the final version typeset using Yourdon's PDP-11/45 and photocomposition equipment, all running under UNIX. We want also to thank the staff and computer operators at Yourdon, Inc. for their expert help and advice.

All or part of a draft of this book was read by Chris Terry, Mark Pearson, Thuy Nguyen, Tom Gibson, and Arden Phillips. We want to express our appreciation to them for the trouble they've taken. We are of course responsible for the contents of this book as it now exists.

---

* Kernighan, Brian W. and Dennis M. Ritchie, *The C Programming Language.* Prentice-Hall, 1978.

† Kernighan, Brian W. and P.J. Plauger, *Software Tools.* Addison-Wesley, 1976.

# Chapter 1
# What C Is

C is a programming language developed at Bell Laboratories around 1972. It was designed and written by one man, Dennis Ritchie, who was then working closely with Ken Thompson on the UNIX operating system. UNIX was conceived as a sort of workshop full of tools for the software engineer, and C turned out to be the most basic tool of all. Nearly every software tool supplied with UNIX, including the operating system and the C compiler, is now written in C.

In the mid-1970s UNIX spread throughout Bell Labs. It was widely licensed to universities. Without any fuss, C began to replace the more familiar languages available on UNIX. No one pushed C. It wasn't made the "official" Bell Labs language. Seemingly self-propelled, without any advertisement, C's reputation spread and its pool of users grew. Ritchie seems to have been rather surprised that so many programmers preferred C to old standbys like Fortran or PL/I, or to new favorites like Pascal and APL. But that's what happened. By 1980 several C compilers were available from independent vendors, and C was running on various non-UNIX systems.

It's entirely in character for C to make such a modest debut. It belongs to a well-established family of languages whose tradition stresses low-key virtues: reliability, regularity, simplicity, ease of use. The members of this family are often called "structured" languages, since they're well suited to *structured programming*, a discipline intended to make programs easier to read and write. Structured programming became something of an ideology in the 1970s, and other languages hew to the party line more closely than C. The prize for purity is often given to Pascal, C's pretty sister. C wasn't meant to win prizes; it was

1

meant to be friendly, capable, and reliable.  Homely virtues these, but quite a few programmers who begin by falling in love with Pascal end up happily married to C.

C's direct ancestry is easy to trace.  This is the line of descent:

Algol 60
*Designed by an international committee, 1960*

↓

CPL
(Combined Programming Language)
*Cambridge and the University of London, 1963*

↓

BCPL
(Basic Combined Programming Language)
*Martin Richards, Cambridge, 1967*

↓

B
*Ken Thompson, Bell Labs, 1970*

↓

C
*Dennis Ritchie, Bell Labs, 1972*

Though Algol appeared only a few years after Fortran, it's a much more sophisticated language, and for that reason has had enormous influence on programming language design.  Its authors paid a great deal of attention to regularity of syntax, modular structure, and other features we tend to think of as "modern."  Unfortunately, Algol never really caught on in the United States, probably because it seemed too abstract, too general.  CPL was an attempt to bring Algol down to earth—in its inventors' words, to "retain contact . . . with the realities of an actual computer"*—a goal shared by C.  Like Algol, CPL was big, with a host of features which did little to enhance its power but did make it hard to learn and difficult to implement.  BCPL aimed to solve the problem by boiling CPL down to its basic good features.  B, written by Ken Thompson for an early implementation of UNIX, is a further

---

* Barron, D.W., Buxton, J.N., Hartley, D.F., Nixon, E., Strachey, C., "The Main Features of CPL." *Computer Journal*, Vol. 6, 1963, p. 134.

simplification of CPL—and a very spare language it is indeed, though well suited for use on the hardware then available. But both BCPL and B carried economy of means so far that they became rather limited languages, useful only when dealing with certain kinds of problems. Ritchie's achievement in C was to restore some of this lost generality, mainly by the cunning use of data types. He managed to do this without sacrificing the simplicity or "computer contact" that were the design goals of CPL.

Like BCPL and B, C has the coherence that's often associated with one-man languages, other well-known examples being Lisp, Pascal, and APL. (Counterexamples include such many-headed monsters as PL/I, Algol 68, and Ada.) Following in his predecessors' small-but-beautiful footsteps, Ritchie was able to avoid the catastrophic complexity of languages that try to be all things to all men. Yet his minimalist approach didn't rob C of its power. By following a few simple, regular rules, C's limited stock of parts can be put together to make more complex parts, which can in turn be put together to form even more elaborate constructions. By way of comparison, think of the complex organic molecules that can be assembled from a dozen different atoms, or the symphonies that have been composed from the twelve notes of the chromatic scale. Simple building blocks (atoms and notes) are put together according to simple rules (of valency and harmony) to build more elaborate parts (radicals, chords) which are in turn used to create complex organisms and music of great beauty.

This ability to build complex programs out of simple elements is C's great strength. If C had a coat of arms, its motto might be *multum in parvo*: a lot from a little.

Languages written by one man usually reflect their author's field of expertise. Dennis Ritchie's field is systems software—computer languages, operating systems, program generators, text processors, etc.—and C is at its best when used to implement tools of this kind. Even though there's a good deal of generality built into C, let's be clear: it's not the language of choice for every application. You can, if you want, use C for writing everything from accounts receivable programs to video games: in principle, almost any computer language can do, one way or another, what any other language can do. And it is true that programs written in C run fast and take little storage space. But while an analysis of variance written in C may run faster than one written in APL, the APL program will be up and running first.

So C's special domain is systems software. Why is it so well suited to that field? Two reasons. First, it's a relatively low-level language that lets you specify every detail in a program's logic to achieve maximum computer efficiency. Second, it's a relatively high-level language that hides the details of the computer's architecture, thus promoting programming efficiency. The key to this paradox is the word *relative*. Relative to what? Or, to put it another way, what *is* C's place in the world of programming languages?

We can answer that question by referring to this hierarchy:

True dialogue

.

.

.

Artificial intelligence "dialogues"
Command languages (as in operating systems)
Problem-oriented languages
Machine-oriented languages
Assembly languages

.

.

.

Hardware

Reading from bottom to top, these categories go from the concrete to the abstract, from the highly detailed to the very general, from machine-oriented to human-oriented, and, more or less, from the past toward the future. The dots represent big leaps, with many steps left out. Early ancestors of the computer, like the Jacquard loom (1805) or Charles Babbage's "analytical engine" (1834), were programmed in hardware, and the day may come when we program a machine by having a chat with it, à la HAL 9000—but that certainly won't happen by the year 2001.

Assembly languages, which provide a fairly painless way for us to work directly with a computer's built-in instruction set, go back to the first days of electronic computers. Since they force you to think in terms of the hardware and to specify every operation in the machine's terms—move these bits into this register and add them to the bits in that other register, then place the result in memory at this location, and so on—they're very tedious to use, and errors are common. The early high-level languages, like Fortran and Algol, were created as alternatives to assembly languages. They were much more general, more abstract, allowing programmers to think in terms of the problem at hand rather than in terms of the computer's hardware. Logical structure could be visibly imposed on the program. It's the difference between writing a = b + c and writing

```
LHLD .c
PUSH H
POP B
LHLD .b
DAD B
SHLD .a
```

which is about the quickest way to say the same thing in the assembly language of the 8080 computer chip.

But the early software designers may have jumped too far up our hierarchy of categories. Algol and Fortran are too abstract for systems-level work; they're *problem-oriented languages*, the sort we use for solving problems in engineering or science or business. Programmers who wanted to write systems software still had to rely on their machine's assembler. After a few years of this drudgery some systems people took a step back, or, in terms of our hierarchy, a step down, and created the category of *machine-oriented languages*. As we saw when we traced C's genealogy, BCPL and B belong to this class of very-low-level software tools. Such languages are excellent for down-on-the-machine programming, but not much use for anything else—they're just too closely wedded to the computer. C is a step above them, and a step below most problem-solving languages, which is what we mean by saying that it's both high- and low-level. It fits into a very cozy niche in the hierarchy, one that somehow feels just right to many software engineers. It's close enough to the computer to give the programmer great control over the details of his program's implementation, yet far enough away that it can ignore the details of the hardware.

## What C Isn't

To begin with, it isn't a language. We call it a language because everyone else does, but the analogy between human speech and programming isn't very apt. C or any other "programming language" is a set of symbols whose possible combinations are precisely defined and which can be used to represent and transform numerically coded values. If that makes C a language then musical notation is a language too, and so is algebra. We know this metaphor has great poetic appeal—math is "the language of science," music is "the universal language"—and we shall speak of "the C language" throughout this book, but understand that we're taking poetic license. Fanciful analogies have a way of hardening into laws of nature.

C isn't a branch of mathematics either, though a C program will often look like something out of an algebra text. Some new programmers stay away from C because it looks like math to them, but that's a nonproblem. You can use C to the full without knowing anything more arcane than a = (b + 1) / c. Because C is a relatively low-level language it knows no higher math. It stays close to the computer, which can handle only very simple arithmetic.

C isn't a religion. Some programming languages are, complete with a priesthood and a flock of disciples. So far C has escaped this kind of silliness, probably because it was designed as a tool for use by professionals who understand that no tool can be perfect.

C isn't perfect. Everyone who works with a tool swears at it sometimes, and you'll find specific criticisms of C scattered throughout this book. We can sum them up in advance by saying that C trades some elegance and some safety features for speed and ease of use. Once you're familiar with the language you'll probably prefer it that way. Since you're not familiar with it yet, we'll help you through the tricky parts.

### Compiling C Programs

If this introduction has done its job, you should be convinced by now that the C language is easily accessible to human beings. Unfortunately, it's not accessible to computers, not directly: a computer can only execute the instructions built into it, instructions that programmers have to deal with at the assembly-language level. To put C into practice we need a program that translates C-language instructions into their machine-level equivalents. Such programs are called *compilers.*

In order to make use of any compiler it is first necessary to write a program in the compiler's language. When we write a program in C, we're writing what is called *source code.* The compiler's job is to take our source code and translate it into instructions that our computer can understand and execute. The compiler's output is called *executable code.* In other words, it's our program in a form that can be directly executed by our computer. Different makes of computers require different versions of the C compiler, since each has its own machine language. The source code always remains the same, but the executable code will change for each computer our program runs on.

The source code passes through a number of intermediate stages before it turns into executable code. We will assume the simplest pos-

sible case: a small program that is complete in itself.  The scenario usually goes like this.  A programmer logs onto his computer and, using
the system editor, writes a program, which he saves as a named file.
This is called the *source code* file.  He then sets the compilation process
in motion by typing some command—in UNIX it's cc.  This action
triggers a whole cascade of translation programs, each of which takes
the user's code, translates it into a lower-level form, and passes that
version along to the next translator.  Here's how we might represent
the cascade graphically:

Write program:            Editor
↓
*C source code*
↓

Compile program:      C preprocessor
↓
*expanded C
source code*
↓

C compiler
↓
*assembly-language
code*
↓

Assembler
↓
*object code
from this program and
library files*
↓

Linker
↓
*executable code*
↓

Run program:           Loader

The *C preprocessor* expands certain shorthand forms in the source code,
as described in Chapter 8.  Its output, the expanded source code, is fed
to the *C compiler* proper.  What comes out of the compiler is the origi-

nal program translated into the computer's native *assembly language.*
This new file is passed along to the system's assembler, which is a program that translates it into a form called *relocatable object code.* Object
code is an intermediate form; it can't be read by the programmer and it
can't be run by the computer. So why bother with it? Because all C
programs must be linked with support routines from the *C run-time
library,* which is described in Chapter 13. The *linker* performs that
chore, linking all the necessary code together and translating it into an
*executable code* file. The programmer can run that code by giving it to
the system's loader, something that's done in UNIX simply by typing
the file's name.

It's a pretty long way, then, from writing a program to running it.
Luckily, we don't really have to think much about the steps involved,
certainly not if we're beginners. The compilation process is hidden
away, at least in UNIX. We merely type cc and wait a few seconds,
wondering why this supposedly fast machine is so slow. At the end of
those seconds we're presented with a runnable program which may or
may not run the way we think it should. If it doesn't, we try to find
the problem in the source code, use the editor to change it, and then
compile it all over again. This happens often.

Let's run through an example. But before we do, we as authors
must face up to a problem that all books on programming languages
encounter. In our examples, what kind of system should we assume
our readers have? The easiest way out, and the most natural, is to
assume that they have exactly the same system we used to write our
examples on: a PDP-11/45 running under Version 6 of UNIX.
Throughout this book we shall refer to this system as our "reference
computer," and to the UNIX/6 version of C as our "reference compiler." If you have access to another version of UNIX, whether Version
7 or System 3, you will find only minor differences between the examples in this book and those run on your computer. If you're using a
non-UNIX version of C, there may be important differences; you
should refer to your user's manual for details.

Now the example. Suppose we want to write a program that
prints the words "Hell is filled with amateur musicians." We first
invoke our system editor and write the source code, which looks like
this:

```
main()
{
    printf("Hell is filled with amateur musicians.\n");
}
```

Now suppose that we have saved this source code under the filename test.c. Here's all we need do to compile and execute the program on our reference computer:*

```
% cc test.c
% a.out
Hell is filled with amateur musicians.
```

The first thing we should mention about this procedure is that the *prompt character* on our reference computer is **%**. (On other UNIX systems it may be **$**.) This prompt must appear at the terminal before we can enter any command. So, following the **%**, we enter the compile command **cc** followed by the name of the source code file:

```
% cc test.c
```

Note that our filename must have the suffix **.c**. This is true of all C source code files. If the suffix is missing, the compilation fails.
Assuming the compilation proceeds smoothly to its conclusion, the system prompt **%** will again appear on the terminal. We can then execute the compiled code by typing **a.out** after the prompt:

```
% a.out
```

and the computer will immediately run the program, displaying the sentence at our terminal:

```
Hell is filled with amateur musicians.
```

If you have been following this procedure on your own machine, and if you now examine your file directory, you will see that your directory contains a new file, **a.out**. You can execute the file **a.out** any time you wish by typing the command **a.out** after the system prompt. The UNIX C compiler always puts its output into the file **a.out**. Of course you can change the file's name to anything you like, and run the program by typing that new name instead of **a.out**.
This is the basic compilation procedure, which should work on practically every UNIX installation just as we've described it. Now for a few variations.

---

* In these and all the other programming examples in this book, all commands are executed only when you depress the carriage-return key after having entered the command. What the user types will always be shown in **boldface**.

Our program was very short, and all the source code was kept in a single file. But real-life C programs are much larger than this example. They almost always consist of a number of separate source files, each of which has been separately compiled and stored in memory under its own filename until the programmer is ready to assemble them into a complete program. As an example of how such a file is compiled and saved, let's use a variant of our previous program. This variant looks similar, but it's not a complete C program—it doesn't have a `main`. (Don't worry about the form of these example programs; all will be explained in good time):

```
print_message()
    {
    printf("Hell is filled with amateur musicians.\n");
    }
```

Assume we again store this source code under the filename `test.c` and then try to compile it:

```
% cc test.c
Undefined:
_main
%
```

We certainly didn't get the output we were expecting. What we got was an error message. If we look at the files in our directory now, we discover that this time we didn't get an `a.out`. However, there is a new file named `test.o`. This is the object code file that corresponds to `test.c`; the `.o` is for "object." The compiler sensed that the program wasn't complete and assumed that we were separately compiling some subsidiary portion of it. It therefore proceeded with the compilation of the program in its usual way but, instead of throwing the object code away after the compilation was complete, as it does when it is dealing with a complete program, it had sense enough to save a copy of the compiled object code.

Suppose we have written and compiled a number of these sub-source files. These will be stored in our computer as object code files. We now want to link them together in order to create our final executable program. The command line for such an assemblage of object code files might look like this:

```
% cc onefile.o twofile.o threefile.o
%
```

Or, if we have several source code files and several object files, we might write:

```
% cc one.c two.o three.c four.o
%
```

Using these procedures, we can write and compile a large program piece by piece, then put all the pieces together. This gives us a chance to debug each piece quickly, without waiting for the whole program to be compiled every time we make a change.

And what will the name of the final, executable program be? a.out, of course. The executable output of the compiler is always stored under the filename a.out. This could be dangerous since any compilation will wipe out an existing a.out file. The solution is obvious. If we want to save an executable file, we must rename it. We could rename it newprog, for example, using the UNIX mv command:

```
% mv a.out newprog
```

Thereafter we can execute the program anytime we wish just by entering its name, newprog, after the prompt.

# Chapter 2
# How C Looks

In this chapter, to give you a feel for C notation, we will look at a typical C program and see how it's compiled and executed under UNIX, the operating system most often associated with C. We won't go into much detail; that is the purpose of the remaining chapters of this primer. If some of the things we say raise questions in your mind that aren't answered here, be patient—the answers will be forthcoming in later chapters.

Let's assume that, using the UNIX editor, we have entered a program into our computer under the filename test.c, which is what we shall call all our sample programs. We can print the source code at our terminal by giving the UNIX command cat test.c. The result is shown at the top of the next page. After test.c has been listed, UNIX lets us know it is waiting for our next command by printing another %. To compile test.c, we enter the command:

```
% cc test.c
```

To execute the compiled program, just type its name:

```
% a.out
```

UNIX will execute the program, which in this case prints the result at the terminal. When execution is done, UNIX again displays the prompt. Here is the complete sequence:

```
% cc test.c
% a.out
mdcclxxvi
%
```

```
% cat test.c

/*
** Program to print 1776 in Roman numerals.
*/
main()
    {
    int a = 1776;

    a = romanize(a, 1000, 'm');
    a = romanize(a, 500, 'd');
    a = romanize(a, 100, 'c');
    a = romanize(a, 50, 'l');
    a = romanize(a, 10, 'x');
    a = romanize(a, 5, 'v');
    romanize(a, 1, 'i');
    putchar('\n');                  /* end with a newline */
    }


/*
** Print the character c as many times as there are
** j's in the number i, then return i minus the j's.
*/
romanize(i, j, c)
char c;
int i, j;
    {
    while(i >= j)
        {
        putchar(c);
        i = i - j;
        }
    return(i);
    }
%
```

---

## How This Program Works

What is this mdcclxxvi? It's the date 1776 in Roman numerals.
All the program does is convert the Arabic number into its Roman
equivalent. The usefulness of such a program is almost nil, of course.
Perhaps someone designing a Fourth of July monument would have a
need for it; but to us the program is very useful because in describing

how it does what it does we can explain many of the characteristics of C programs in general.

As you might guess from looking at `test.c`, it works by a process of continued subtractions. It begins by attempting to subtract 1000 from 1776. As often as this subtraction can be performed successfully, the program prints the Roman numeral m. That only happens once, of course, since the remainder of 1776 minus 1000 is 776. The program next subtracts 500 from 776 as many times as possible, printing the Roman numeral d for every successful subtraction. This subtraction too can be performed only once, since 776 minus 500 is 276. And so it goes, the program printing c's, l's, x's, v's and i's as it subtracts hundreds, fifties, tens, fives and ones until there's nothing left. And that's it.

## C Functions

All this work gets done within two *functions,* which are the basic operational entities of any C program. Every C program is put together from one or more functions, each of which performs some necessary task in the program. In our sample program the functions are `main` and `romanize`. `main` starts things off and masterminds the program by giving the order in which the subtractions occur. `romanize` performs the actual subtractions, making use of `putchar`, which is a *library* function that causes characters to be printed at the terminal. (We will discuss C's library functions, including `putchar`, in Chapter 13.)

Each of these C functions is an independent entity. Indeed, all C functions are created equal, but one is more equal than the others—the function `main` is always executed first.

## Function Definitions

There are dozens of standardized library functions like `putchar` that perform useful chores, but of course the interesting functions are those we define ourselves. Every function we write must be defined before it can be used—indeed, the act of writing the function is the act of defining it, since what we write is called the *function definition.*

Function definitions are what make up most of the "code" (that is, source code) written by C programmers. A function definition has two parts, a *function header* and a *body.* Reasonably enough, the header sits atop the body. The header defines the function's name and arguments; the body defines what the function does.

Let's look more closely at the function `romanize` in the source code file `test.c`. Short as it is, it has the claws and teeth of a real live function. Remember, the whole thing looks like this:

```
/*
** Print the character c as many times as there are
** j's in the number i, then return i minus the j's.
*/
romanize(i, j, c)
char c;
int i, j;
    {
    while(i >= j)
        {
        putchar(c);
        i = i - j;
        }
    return(i);
    }
```

Notice that the function definition is crowned by a *comment:*

```
/*
** Print the character c as many times as there are
** j's in the number i, then return i minus the j's.
*/
```

Anything between a `/*` and a matching `*/` is ignored by the C compiler. This allows us to write comments to ourselves, or for programmers who may inherit our code. Comments can cover several lines, like the one above, or they can be one-liners like the comment

```
/* end with a newline */
```

in the function `main`. Long or short, comments have no effect whatever on the size or speed of the final program. Use them liberally; write them as if the compiler *could* read them. In particular, no function definition should be considered complete without a comment that tells what that function does.

Now back to the function definition. `romanize`'s function header is

```
romanize(i, j, c)
char c;
int i, j;
```

The first line names the function and, within the parens, lists its *formal arguments,* which we'll discuss later in this chapter. For the moment think of these arguments as containers for data, little buckets that are used to pass information into the function. The second and third lines of the header tell the compiler more about these arguments—to round out our metaphor, they specify the size of the buckets. Here's the jargon we shall use for these parts of the function's anatomy: `romanize` is the function's *name;* `(i, j, c)` is its *argument list;* and `char c;` and `int i, j;` are its *argument declarations.*

Notice that `main`'s argument list is empty. It has no formal arguments at all, which is perfectly OK; there's no rule that says a function has to take arguments. In such a case the function may define its own data internally or get data from an outside source—the user's keyboard, for example, or a disk file.

The body of a C function contains the executable code; it is where the work gets done. The body of `romanize` is

```
{
while (i >= j)
   {
   putchar(c);
   i = i - j;
   }
return(i);
}
```

The lines ending in semicolons, like `i = i - j;`, are *statements.* We can put two or more such statements together inside a pair of curly braces to form a compound statement, or *block,* as we have done with

```
{
putchar(c);
i = i - j;
}
```

The braces tell the compiler that these lines must be treated as a unit. In this particular context, the braces indicate that the two statements are to be executed over and over as long as—while—the *condition* (i >= j) remains true.

Naturally, any program needs data to chew on.  In our example there are several different kinds of data.  There are *constants* like 1776, 1000 and 'm', and there's one *variable,* the a in main.  In general, variables are named values which may change as the program runs.  Variables like a must be assigned a value before they can be used, just as a cup must be filled before you can drink from it.  (There are also the formal arguments we've already mentioned, i, j, and c, which are variables of a special kind.  Formal arguments, as we'll soon see, take their values from the *actual arguments* in a *function call.*)

Notice that main's variable a appears in a special statement before it's put to any use:

```
int a = 1776;
```

This is a *declaration statement* which happens also to *initialize* a to the value 1776.  It looks much like the argument declarations int i, j, but those occur in the header of the function romanize, while a's declaration appears in main's body.  Declarations are discussed fully beginning in the next chapter; at this stage the important thing for you to note is that every variable (and every argument) must be *declared* before you can do anything at all with it in C.

C's *operators* are easily distinguished because they have a fixed form that consists of neither letters nor digits.  Here is the complete list:

| | | | | |
|---|---|---|---|---|
| + | & | \ | ^ | ¦ |
| ? : | -- | / | == | > |
| >= | ++ | != | << | < |
| <= | && | ! | ¦¦ | % |
| ~ | >> | -> | - | = |

A strange looking lot.  Some of the operators, like the ?  : combination, are unique to C.  Others, like + and =, look familiar (didn't I see them once or twice in an algebra class?)—but appearances are deceptive and you shouldn't take anything for granted.  The analogy between C's operators and the symbols of everyday arithmetic can be treacherous.

The braces help the compiler determine the order in which it will execute the statements.  For example, what happens in

```
while (i >= j)
   {
   putchar(c);
   i = i - j;
   }
```

is quite different from what happens in

```
while (i >= j)
   {
   putchar(c);
   }
i = i - j;
```

Which brings up the question of where to put the braces on the page, and how to indent the lines of code in a C function's definition. While the presence or absence of braces is crucial to the correct execution of a program, their placement on the page is totally a matter of taste because C has *free-form* syntax. That is, unless they are in quotes, or used to separate two names, blanks—and tabs and carriage returns as well—are ignored by the compiler, which means our sample program could just as well have been written this way:

```
% cat test.c
main(){int a=1776;a=romanize(a,1000,'m');a=
romanize(a,500,'d');a=romanize(a,100,'c');a
=romanize(a,50,'l');a=romanize(a,10,'x');a
=romanize(a,5,'v');romanize(a,1,'i');putchar
('\n');}romanize(i,j,c)char c;int i,j;{while
(i>=j){putchar(c);i=i-j;}return(i);}
% cc test.c
% a.out
mdcclxxvi
%
```

This makes exactly as much sense to the C compiler as the first version of our example program, though it probably makes much less sense to you. We will continue to use the style shown in our original program. Here are two popular alternatives, each shown with the source code for romanize:

```
romanize(i, j, c)
char c;
int i, j;
{
   while (i >= j)
   {
      putchar(c);
      i = i - j;
   }
   return(i);
}
```

and

```
romanize(i, j, c)
char c;
int i, j;
{
   while (i >= j) {
      putchar(c);
      i = i - j;
   }
   return(i);
}
```

If you prefer either of these, or perhaps some other style of indentation and locating braces, that's fine.  Just be consistent.

### Names, Names, Names

All the names used in a C program for constants, variables, or functions follow the same rules: the names are made up of letters and digits, and the first character in a name must be a letter.  The underscore _ can also serve as a letter; it helps separate the parts of long descriptive names, since blanks inside names aren't legal.  (So *interest to date* can become the variable interest_to_date, etc.) Letters in upper case are not equivalent to the same letters in lower case. VELOCITY, Velocity and velocity are all different names.  A name may have any number of characters, but only the first eight are retained by the C compiler.  That is, to the compiler the names honorific and honorificabilitudinatatibus are the same thing, and so are the names interest_paid and interest_payable.  (The number of characters in file names will vary with the operating system. You had best check what your operating system requires.)

Whatever the names you use in your programs, they should be as descriptive as possible. The name of a function or of a variable should tell you what the function does or what the variable represents, even if it means using names having more than eight characters.

And what about the name we've called our program: `test.c`? This is the name of the source code file; as such, it belongs to the operating system, not to C. For the rules to follow in naming files, go to your operating system's documentation. (However, most compilers insist that all C source code files must end in the suffix `.c`.)

There's one more thing you must watch out for. The names you use must not match any of C's *reserved words*:

```
auto        double      if          static
break       else        int         struct
case        entry       long        switch
char        extern      register    typedef
continue    for         return      union
default     float       short       unsigned
do          goto        sizeof      while
```

These words have special meaning to the compiler. We will explain the use of most of them as we go along; for now just remember not to use them as function or variable names in your programs.

We've said that functions are completely independent. Then how do `main` and `romanize` communicate with one another? The answer is that they pass data back and forth in the form of *arguments* and *returned values*. This is easier to show than tell.

Let's run through our program and hand-execute some of it just as C would. Program execution begins with `main`, of course. The first statement in `main` is

```
int a = 1776;
```

which declares the variable `a` and assigns it the initial value `1776`. The next statement is

```
a = romanize(a, 1000, 'm');
```

in which `a` is a variable name, `1000` is a numeric constant, and `'m'` is a character constant representing a well-known letter of the alphabet. Notice that these actual arguments appear inside the parens that follow the function name, just as `romanize`'s formal arguments do in its argument list: `(i, j, c)`. The correspondence between actual and formal arguments is exact. Continuing our bucket analogy:

> the value in **a** goes into the bucket labeled `i`
> `1000` goes into the bucket labeled `j`
> `'m'` goes into the bucket labeled `c`

The expression `romanize(a, 1000, 'm')` is an example of a *function call;* when this point is reached in the program, the flow of control is shunted from `main` to `romanize`. At the same moment, the actual argument values `1776`, `'m'`, and `1000` are copied into the formal arguments `i`, `j`, and `c`. That is, the little buckets in our analogy are filled with data. The statements in the body of `romanize` can now be executed using the data copied from `main`. `romanize` prints `'m'` as many times as there are `1000`'s in `1776`, then returns `1776` minus `1000`—in other words, `romanize` returns `776`. When the `return` statement is executed, it shunts us back to the spot in `main` from which we jumped to `romanize`. But we don't come back empty-handed. We return with the value `776`, which replaces the original function call. That is, the original statement in `main`

```
a = romanize(a, 1000, 'm');
```

is equivalent to

```
a = the value returned by romanize(a, 1000, 'm');
```

or

```
a = 776;
```

So a's value has been changed from `1776` to `776`. Therefore, when the next statement in `main` is executed:

```
a = romanize(a, 500, 'd');
```

it is the value `776` in **a** that is passed to `romanize`.

It doesn't take much familiarity with C to realize that the successive calls to `romanize` pare down a's value from 1776 to 776 to 276 to 76 to 26 to 6 and finally to 1. So one of `romanize`'s jobs, for which it uses `putchar`, is to print out its third argument `c` for as many times as its second argument `j` is contained in its first argument `i`. `romanize` also has the job of returning the new value of `i` to `main`.

It's clear that `main` doesn't really do anything but call `romanize` time after time with the appropriate actual arguments and, at the end of everything, call `putchar` to print the special character `'\n'`, which sends a *newline* (i.e., carriage return and linefeed) to the user's terminal. (For more on special characters like `'\n'`, see the next chapter.)

## More on Compiling

In our example the two functions are kept in one source file, and in principle there's no reason why all the functions in a program can't be kept in the same file and compiled at the same time. This is neat and tidy as long as the amount of source code involved is fairly small—say fewer than a dozen files. It takes a relatively long time to compile all the functions in a large program. That wouldn't be so bad if the program were compiled only once, but this isn't the way that programs get written. In the process of writing and debugging a program it is usually compiled again and again and again. To save time, therefore, the programmer will separate the functions into fairly small groups of related functions so he can test and change the code in that group and then have to recompile only that group. When he's ready to try his entire program, he can then link that group to the other groups which have been compiled. Since the example we are using is made up of two functions, we can use it to show how functions may be compiled separately. Suppose we break the program up into two files called `test1.c` and `test2.c`, as shown on the next page. Now if we want to compile the two source code files at the same time we write after the prompt:

```
% cc test1.c test2.c
```

The compiler goes to work, compiling first `test1.c`, then `test2.c`. As it finishes with each, it lists the file's name on the terminal:

```
test1.c:
test2.c:
```

```
% cat test1.c

/*
** Program to print 1776 in Roman numerals.
*/
main()
    {
    int a = 1776;

    a = romanize(a, 1000, 'm');
    a = romanize(a, 500, 'd');
    a = romanize(a, 100, 'c'),
    a = romanize(a, 50, 'l');
    a = romanize(a, 10, 'x');
    a = romanize(a, 5, 'v');
    romanize(a, 1, 'i');
    putchar('\n');                 /* end with a newline */
    }

% cat test2.c

/*
** Print the character c as many times as there are
** j's in the number i, then return i minus the j's.
*/
romanize(i, j, c)
char c;
int i, j;
    {
    while(i >= j)
        {
        putchar(c);
        i = i - j;
        }
    return(i);
    }
%
```

When it is finished with the last file, it prints the system prompt again.
We can then run these two executable files at the same time by typing
the command a.out after the prompt, as before:

```
% a.out
```

and the program will be executed:

```
mdcclxxvi
%
```

It's a bit unusual to compile more than one source code file at a time. More typically, a C programmer will first compile the source code files containing ancillary functions, then link them together with the source code file containing `main`. (`main` is usually the organizer and driver of a group of related functions, as in our example program.)

```
% cc test2.c
Undefined:
_main
%
```

The message `Undefined: _main` tells us that no main function was defined. That's all right; we'll supply that lack when we compile the source code file containing `main`:

```
% cc test1.c test2.o
% a.out
mdcclxxvi
%
```

(Remember, compiling *filename*.c creates *filename*.o, the equivalent object code file. Object code files are linked to create the executable code module named `a.out`.)

The examples we've shown so far may not make a very convincing case for separate compilation, but that's because we haven't written a very general program. Simply turning `1776` into `mdcclxxvi` is a silly, one-shot job. Let's cast our program into a more general form. Suppose we rewrite it as follows:

```
% cat test2.c

/*
** Print an Arabic number in Roman numerals.
*/
roman(arabic)
int arabic;
    {
    arabic = romanize(arabic, 1000, 'm');
    arabic = romanize(arabic, 500, 'd');
    arabic = romanize(arabic, 100, 'c');
    arabic = romanize(arabic, 50, 'l');
    arabic = romanize(arabic, 10, 'x');
    arabic = romanize(arabic, 5, 'v');
    romanize(arabic, 1, 'i');
    putchar('\n');              /* end with a newline */
    }


/*
** Print the character c as many times as there are
** j's in the number i, then return i minus the j's.
*/
romanize(i, j, c)
char c;
int i, j;
    {
    while(i >= j)
        {
        putchar(c);
        i = i - j;
        }
    return(i);
    }

% cc test2.c
Undefined:
_main
%
```

As before, when we compiled `test2.c` we got an error message that tells us our program doesn't have a `main` function; we'll supply one in a moment.

By now you should know enough about C to understand what the changes do.  While `romanize` is unchanged, `main` has been generalized to `roman`, a function that takes an integer argument and prints it as a Roman numeral. A function such as this could actually be useful occasionally, so we've compiled it to keep in a library of useful functions. We can exercise it by writing a function `main` that supplies a series of integers to `roman`:

```
% cat test1.c

/*
** Print numbers from 1 to 25 as Roman numerals.
*/
main()
  {
    int x = 1;

    while (x <= 25)
       {
       roman(x);
       x = x + 1;
       }
    }
%
```

As you see on the next page, compiling the new `test1.c` and linking it to `test2.o` has given us a runnable `a.out`. If something about these results looks odd to you, it's probably because you're more accustomed to seeing iv, ix, xiv, xix and xxiv than you are to seeing the forms more commonly used by the Romans—iiii, viiii, xiiii, xviiii and xxiiii. But it would also take a more complicated program to handle the subtractive notation. Perhaps when you've finished this primer you may want to try writing such a program as an exercise.

A final note about separate compilation. You needn't put up with the `Undefined: _main` error message every time you compile a `main`-less source code file if you don't want to. That message comes from the linker. If you enter the compile command using what is called the `-c` option:

```
% cc -c test2.c
%
```

the linking step in the compilation procedure will be skipped and the error message won't appear, while the object code will go into `test2.o` as it did before.

```
% cc test1.c test2.o
% a.out
i
ii
iii
iiii
v
vi
vii
viii
viiii
x
xi
xii
xiii
xiiii
xv
xvi
xvii
xviii
xviiii
xx
xxi
xxii
xxiii
xxiiii
xxv
%
```

# Chapter 3
# Primary Data Types

"Data" is an extremely common word in the programmer's kit of handy, easy-to-use jargon. It is almost impossible for a programmer to talk for two minutes about computing without saying "data" in one context or another. There are *data types*, *data objects*, *data checking*, *data bases*, *data flow*, *data sets*, and so on—all of which are part of *data processing*, whatever that is. Though the word is used very often, it is seldom defined; many of us can't even agree whether "data" is plural (*we* think it is) or singular (it's a free country).

We will use the term *data* in this book to mean something very specific. For us, data refers to the actual values in a program, which can be either *constants* or *variables*. Constants are, or have, fixed values; they never change. Variable values can vary, of course. As we have seen, variables are usually given descriptive names of some kind, like the well-known "velocity" and "acceleration" in physics problems that can assume different values at different instants of time. In the same way, the variable names in a computer program can take on different values at different instants of time as the program runs.

In C there are two fundamentally different types of data value— *integer* and *floating point*. From these two we can spin off two other primary data types— *character* and *double precision*, which gives us a total of four. Almost all the data values you use in your C programs will be either integers or characters. The other two have little to do with the kind of programming C was designed for, so we shall only touch on them briefly in this chapter.

To users of high-horsepower languages like PL/I it may seem odd that C programmers should be able to make do with such a tiny stable

28

of data types. However, as we shall see in later chapters, C people aren't really deprived. Many other data types can be derived from C's basic four; in fact, the number of derived and defined types is theoretically unlimited. The C programmer who needs them can invent whatever data types he wants. This is another example of the language's modular architecture. By following a few regular rules, small, simple units can be put together to form very elaborate constructions.

## Integers

An integer is a whole number like 1 or 2 or 3 or −1 or 0 that doesn't have a fractional part. An integer may have a positive or negative value. Our reference C compiler can handle integer values from −32768 through +32767.

Integer *constants* are written just as they are in everyday arithmetic. Zero is 0, the number one is 1 (but not + 1, which is illegal in C), and minus one is − 1 (the minus sign always being present in a negative value).

Integer constants are not declared before they are used but integer *variables* must always be. The *declaration*, which is placed at the top of a block, looks like this:

```
{
int a ;
int b ;
int c ;
    .
    .
    .

}
```

or, declaring several variables at the same time, like this:

```
{
int a, b, c ;
    .
    .
    .

}
```

or, using more meaningful variable names, like this:

```
{
int graduating_class, rank, student_number;
   .
   .
   .

}
```

(The curly braces are shown to emphasize that declarations go at the top of a block of code; we won't use them again in this chapter.)

The magic word, the *keyword*, used to declare an integer variable is `int`. Once a variable has been declared as `int`, it can be assigned an integer value by the *assignment operator* = , as in

```
int graduating_class, rank, student_number;
   .
   .
   .
student_number = 31670;
rank = 473;
graduating_class = 1985;
```

Its use should be clear from the context. In this example, the values to the right of the symbol = are assigned to the variable names on their left. The variable named `student_number` is assigned the integer value `31670`, the variable `rank` is assigned the integer value `473`, and so forth. We caution you not to think of the = here as being anything at all like the equal sign = in mathematics, despite their similar form and deceptively similar use. True, `student_number` is set "equal to" `31670`, `rank` is set "equal to" `473`, etc., but the = symbolizes the operation of assigning the constants to the variable names; it is *not* a statement of equality, and the expression $x = x + 1$ is perfectly legal—it simply increments the value of $x$ by one.

As our example suggests, variables can be declared in any order. In particular, their order of declaration need not match the order in which they appear later in the block of code.

We've said that integers in our reference C compiler can't have values less than −32768 or greater than +32767. The programming you do in C will seldom strain these fairly generous limits, but larger integers are available if you should need them. C offers a variation of the integer data type that will provide what are called *long* integer

values. Long integer variables must be declared using the keyword
`long`:

```
long int head_count;
```

Think of `long` as an adjective that modifies the `int` being declared.

The use of long integers requires a little more space in memory
and the program may run a bit slower, but the range of values you can
use is expanded enormously. In our reference compiler, the value of a
long integer (familiarly called a "long") can range from −2147483648
through +2147483647. More than this you shouldn't need unless
you're taking a world census.

## Characters

Like integer data types, character data types may be either constants or
variables. Character variables are declared using the keyword `char` at
the beginning of a block:

```
char sex, party;
```

Character constants are written as letters or symbols inside single quotation marks:

```
char sex, party;
   .
   .
   .
sex = 'f';
party = 'd';
```

In this illustration, `sex` and `party` are first declared as character variables; they are then assigned the constant values `'f'` and `'d'`,
respectively. Now, we sort of intuitively know what it means to say
that the integer variable **x** takes on the value 1 or 2 or 3, but how can
`'f'` or `'d'` be values? What exactly is a "character value," either
constant or variable? Characters in C *are* in fact numeric values, but
they are values we have agreed to associate with the letters of the
alphabet. This range of values has been determined by the amount of
space that any given make of computer has allotted for the coding of
characters. In other words, we are using a simple transformation code
that associates what we call character values with certain integer values.

Many of us are familiar with codes of this kind from childhood games of one sort or another: "If we agree A is 1 and B is 2, and so on, then the secret message 8, 9, 20, 8, 5, 18, 5 is . . ." The transformation code used by our reference compiler is the American Standard Code for Information Interchange, or ASCII (pronounced to rhyme with Lasky). In ASCII the capital letter 'A' is 65, 'B' is 66, and so on, the small letter 'a' is 97, 'b' is 98, and so on, and there are also numbers for such things as numerals, spaces, tabs, carriage returns, and a zero for null—i.e., nothing at all.  So the secret message becomes, in ASCII, 72, 73, 32, 84, 72, 69, 82, 69 . . . the principle is exactly the same.* The use of integers to represent characters makes char and int values interchangeable in many situations.  (But there is no necessary relationship between the *symbols* '1', '2', . . .'9' and the *integers* used to represent them.  In ASCII '0' has the value 48, '1' has the value 49, and so forth.)

### Escape Sequences

We've said that character constants are written in the form 'M' or 'm' or '%' or ' ' (for a space), but what about special characters like the carriage return or the backspace?  How do we write these into a C program?  There are several ways of doing so.  For the most common special characters, C provides what are called *escape sequences*—the backslash character \ followed by a letter.  The backslash \ signals the compiler that the letter which follows it has special significance.  The escape sequences defined for C are:

| | |
|---|---|
| \n | newline (i.e., linefeed—carriage return) |
| \t | tab |
| \b | backspace |
| \r | carriage return |
| \f | form feed |
| \\ | backslash |
| \' | single quote |
| \0 | null |

Thus we can write the declaration

```
char linefeed;
    .
    .
    .
    linefeed = '\n';
```

---

* The 32 is an ASCII blank.

in order to give the variable called `linefeed` the value of a newline character constant.  Note that the escape sequence \n is a *single* character that happens to be symbolized by two keystrokes; the same is true of all the other escape sequences.

Escape sequences can be mixed freely with other characters.  For example the C statement

```
printf("A\nBC\nDEF\n");
```

generates the output

```
A
BC
DEF
```

when the program is run.  (`printf` is a library routine which prints whatever it finds between the quotation marks " ".  More on `printf` in Chapter 13.)

As for those characters not defined by an escape sequence, we did say they were integers and it's perfectly acceptable to use integer constants to define them.  For example, the ASCII code defines the value of a bell character (which causes some terminals to beep and others to ring a bell) as 7, and we can use this value directly to identify the variable name `bell` as a bell character in our programs:

```
char bell;
   .
   .
   .
bell = 7;
```

Now we need only write the expression `putchar(bell)` at the appropriate points in our program to get the user's attention with a beep or a ring; it makes a good attention-getter.  However, when possible you should use escape sequences and not numeric constants to identify nonprinting characters.  Escape sequences are more general and are, therefore, portable from one coding system to another.

### Floating Point

Floating-point data play no big part in the kind of programming C was really meant for.  C is at its best in systems work—writing interpreters, compilers, operating systems, editors, and such.  In those contexts floating-point arithmetic is nearly useless. Still, programmers at some installations do use C for data reduction, statistical analysis, linear programming, and other number-crunching applications which definitely call for floating point, and the language has a fully developed floating-point capability.

Floating-point data values are approximations of *real numbers,* numbers usually expressed as decimal fractions like 2.71828 or 3.14159 or 0.01745. Real numbers that are very large or very small are often written in exponential or "scientific" notation. For example, Avogadro's number, 602000000000000000000000.0, may be written as $6.02 \times 10^{23}$ (6.02 times ten to the twenty-third power). Planck's constant, 0.000000000000000000000000006626 erg-second, is more easily written as $6.626 \times 10^{-27}$ erg-second (6.626 times ten to the minus twenty-seventh power). Either the decimal fraction or the exponential style is acceptable for writing floating-point constants in C, but with a slight change in the exponential notation. Because we can't do superscripts on most computer terminals, $6.02 \times 10^{23}$ must instead be written as `6.02e23` or `6.02E23` or `6.02e+23`. (Either an e or an E will do.) Similarly, $6.626 \times 10^{-27}$ becomes `6.626e-27`. The e or E stands for *exponent* and is followed by the power of ten involved.

Though programmers usually avoid the E-notation unless a constant is very large or very small, C stores all floating-point numbers internally in an exponental form, no matter what their magnitude. The messy details are beyond the scope of a primer, and don't concern C programmers directly; but it's important to realize that floating point puts a good deal more overhead on the software and hardware than do character and integer data types.

The keyword used to declare a floating-point variable is `float`:

```
float x, y, z;
    .
    .
    .
x = 12.345;
y = .12345e2;
z = 12345.0e-3;
```

The above example shows three different ways of assigning the same floating-point constant to the variables **x**, **y**, and **z**.

In our standard C compiler, floating-point values range from around ±2.9387e−39 to about ±1.7014e+38, with about six places of accuracy for the mantissa (i.e., the digits to the left of the e or **E**).

Notice we said *around* and *about.* In floating point, everything is approximate, and errors accumulate quickly. You can minimize this problem, at some additional cost in speed and program size, by resorting to our fourth primary data type, *double precision.*

## Double Precision

A double-precision value is simply a floating-point value specified with greater exactness; it requires twice as much storage space as `float`. The use of double precision isn't guaranteed to double the number of significant digits in your results, but it does greatly improve the accuracy of the arithmetic and reduces the accumulation of rounding errors. Results will vary from one machine to another, but as an experiment we tried a little simple arithmetic on our reference computer. Two variables were declared, `x` as a `float` and `y` as a `double`. Both were set to 0.0, then added to 100000.0 ten thousand times, and finally divided by 10000.0. The final value of `y` was what we would expect it to be: 100000.000000. But `x` turned out to be 100014.820313. So `x` was in error by .015 percent or thereabouts—a small percentage if you're balancing your checkbook, but enough to miss the moon in a space shot.

Double-precision variables are declared using the keyword `double`:

```
double logE, sin_per_sec;
   .
   .
   .
logE = 2.718281828459;
sin_per_sec = 4.848136811076e-7;
```

As you see, double-precision constants use the same exponential notation as single-precision floating-point constants; the only difference is in the number of significant digits that can be assigned. All real-number constants are handled as double-precision by the compiler.

## Initializing Variables

We've shown quite a few examples in which a variable is first declared and later given a value, e.g.,

```
double logE;
   .
   .
   .
logE = 2.718281828459;
```

Wherever we know that we want to start off by giving a variable a certain initial value, we can combine these two operations in an initialization procedure like this one:

```
double logE = 2.718281828459;
```

Floats, integers, and characters are initialized in similar ways:

```
float x = 12.345;
int rank = 473;
char sex = 'f';
```

Each initialization works for one variable only; for instance,

```
float x, y, z = 12.345;
```

is exactly equivalent to

```
float x;
float y;
float z = 12.345;
```

Both initialize z but not x and not y.

# Chapter 4
# Storage Classes

We said in the last chapter that every data value, whether variable or constant, has a data type. If a value is a variable, its data type must be declared. Constants need not be declared because their data type is apparent from their appearance (e.g., 1 or 1.0 or '1').

We've really said all that needs to be said about constants, but we're not finished with variables. Not only do all variables have a data type, they also have a *storage class*. We haven't mentioned storage classes yet, even though we've given several examples of runnable C programs in which storage classes do play their part. We were able to get away with this because storage classes, unlike data types, have *defaults*. If a variable's storage class is not specified in its declaration, the compiler will assume you want the storage class that is implied by the context.*

What's in a name? From the C compiler's point of view, a variable name simply identifies some physical location within the computer where a string of bits representing the variable's current value will be stored. There are basically two kinds of locations in a computer where such a value may be kept: in memory or in one of the cpu registers. It

---

* This assignment of storage classes by default points up the fact that C is a pragmatic language rather than a theoretically exact language. The author of C wanted the language to be used, and he knew that users quickly get tired of specifying every little thing in detail. So he let a few rules slide. A truly rigorous approach would admit no defaults, and it may be that this is the way you would prefer to write C programs. If so, you can write your programs more methodically than the compiler requires by always making sure to specify your variables' storage class.

is a variable's storage class which determines whether it is being stored in memory or in a register. More subtly, a variable's storage class also tells *when* it is active—that is, its storage class specifies the variable's *scope.* This explanation begs the question, but we'll get into scope shortly.

There are four storage classes in C: *automatic, register, static* and *external,* with *register* being a variant of *automatic.*

## Automatic Variables

The declaration of *automatic* variables looks like this:

```
{
auto int a ;
auto int b = 12345 ;
auto char c ;
auto float d = 123.45 ;
   .
   .
   .
}
```

However, it should be understood that while the keyword `auto` *may* be used to declare automatic variables, its use is not obligatory. In fact, this particular keyword almost never appears in workaday C code. Whenever a variable is declared inside a block (usually at the beginning of a function) and no explicit storage class is given, the variable is assumed to be automatic. Most variables do fall into this category.

An automatic variable's *scope* is limited to the block in which it appears. As long as that block, or any block subsumed within that block, is being executed, the variable exists and can be referenced. As soon as the program leaves that block, the variable ceases to exist. Now you see it, now you don't. Since "exists" in this sense means "occupies a place within the computer," automatic variables have an obvious appeal: they don't take up room when they're not actually needed. There's another appealing feature that may be less obvious. Since automatic variables are local to a given function, their value can't be changed accidentally by what happens in some other function. Making variables automatic keeps them out of harm's way.

The following example, even though it doesn't run, will illustrate what we mean by the scope of an automatic variable. There are three blocks in the example, each enclosed by a pair of braces. The outer block (effectively the whole program) contains two inner blocks. x is

an automatic variable; it is declared at the head of the outer block and
therefore exists throughout the function `main`. The fact that it persists throughout `main` naturally means it's active in both of the inner
blocks too.

```
% cat test.c

main()
  {
  /* beginning of outer block */
  int x = 1;

    {
    /* inner block #1 */

    int y = 2;

    printf("%d %d\n", x, y);
    }


    {
    /* inner block #2 */
    printf("%d %d\n", x, y);   /* this is line 16 */
    }

  printf("%d %d\n", x, y);   /* and this is line 19 */
  /* end of outer block */
  }

% cc test.c
test.c:16: y undefined; func. main
test.c:19: y undefined; func. main
%
```

On the other hand, the variable **y** is declared at the head of the
first of the inner blocks. It too is an automatic variable. **y**, however,
lives only within its own block. Its scope does not include the outermost block or the second of the inner blocks. The result: error mes-
sages telling us that the variable **y** is undefined in lines 16 and 19 of
the function `main`, which is where we want the program to print the
values of **y** in the second and third `printf` statements. In other
words, the compiler is telling us that **y** is undefined outside the first
inner loop. Notice, though, that the variable **x** is OK everywhere, since
it's defined in the outer block that subsumes the two inner blocks.

An interesting consequence of this local-scope business is that we can use the same variable name for different automatic variables in different blocks without confusing the compiler, though we ourselves may well become hopelessly confused.  How can we explain the result we get when we run this next program?

```
% cat test.c

main( )
    {
    int x = 1;
      {
      int x = 2;
        {
        int x = 3;
        printf("%d\n", x);
        }
      printf("%d\n", x);
      }
    printf("%d\n", x);
    }

% cc test.c
% a.out
3
2
1
%
```

The x defined in the outermost block is initialized to 1; the x defined in the middle block is initialized to 2; and the x defined in the inner block is initialized to 3.  When the outer block is active, x will be 1; but when the middle block is active, the outer block's x is temporarily put on the shelf and the new, local x (which is valued at 2) takes over; and when the inner block is active, the first two x values are both on the shelf and the inner x, which is valued at 3, takes over.  As soon as the inner block is finished, the middle block's x (with its value of 2) takes over again; as soon as *it's* done, the original x (with its value of 1) takes over.

Note that we could have written the program with the keyword auto included in every declaration:

```
% cat test.c

main()
  {
  auto int x = 1;
    {
    auto int x = 2;
      {
      auto int x = 3;
      printf("%d\n", x);
      }
    printf("%d\n", x);
    }
  printf("%d\n", x);
  }

% cc test.c
% a.out
3
2
1
%
```

But omitting `auto` made no difference, since variables declared inside functions are always automatic unless otherwise specified.

Note also that we've been initializing our automatic variables as we declare them. The definition of the C language says you can initialize an automatic variable at the time you declare it if its data type is one of the primary types discussed in Chapter 3: `char`, `int`, `float`, `double`.* In fact, if you *don't* initialize an automatic variable you must assume its contents to be garbage until you give it a value. For example:

---

* But, as we shall see in Chapters 9 and 12, you cannot initialize an automatic array or structure.

```
% cat test.c

main()
  {
  int x;
    {
    int x;
      {
      int x = 3;
      printf("%d\n", x);
      }
    printf("%d\n", x);
    }
  printf("%d\n", x);
  }

% cc test.c
% a.out
3
0
850
%
```

What happened? Well, **x** is declared but not initialized in the outer block; it is declared but not initialized in the middle block; and it is declared *and* initialized in the inner block. So when we print the value of **x** in the inner block we get 3; but when we leave that block, the inner **x**—and its value—vanishes, while the middle and outer **x**'s (which are completely different variables, remember, though we are calling all three "**x**") have unpredictable values which turn out to be garbage—in this case 0 and 850, respectively.

When you specify an initial value for an automatic variable, that value is assigned to that variable *each time the block in which the variable is active is executed.* Remember, an initialization like:

```
{
int x = 1;
    .
    .
    .

}
```

is exactly equivalent to

```
{
int x;
x = 1;
    .

    .

    .

}
```

The first form is just shorthand for the second.

Before continuing we should emphasize that the last few examples we have been using are highly artificial. Very few C programmers ever declare variables anywhere except at the beginning of a function; to do otherwise is a dangerous practice. But we wanted to emphasize that automatic variables are *local* to the block in which they are declared, even when that block is nested within another block.

Suppose we rewrite the program shown on page 40 in such a way that the declarations are located at the beginning of independent functions:*

```
% cat test.c

main()
   {
   int x = 1;

   middle();
   printf("%d\n", x);
   }

inner()
   {
   int x = 3;

   printf("%d\n", x);
   }
```

---

* Note that the functions in this program are listed in alphabetical order, except for main(). That's a practice we'll follow throughout the rest of this primer for the sake of uniformity and also to show the order of the functions in a program is unimportant. C itself doesn't require that functions be in any particular order.

```
middle()
    {
    int x = 2;

    inner();
    printf("%d\n", x);
    }

% cc test.c
% a.out
3
2
1
%
```

Here the three blocks have been replaced by three functions. Just as the outer block of our example on page 40 contains a middle block which in turn contains the inner block, this program's `main` function calls the `middle` function which in turn calls the `inner` function. Again, the three x-variables are local to their own blocks (in this case to their own functions).

However, this analogy between the middle and inner blocks of a single function and the independent functions `middle` and `inner` is only superficial. It would be wrong to say that any C function "contains" another in the way that a set of Chinese boxes can be nested together. True, the function `main` calls the function `middle` and `middle` calls the function `inner`; but the important point is that no C function can be *defined* inside another function. All C functions are equal. As we said earlier, the variables defined in the outer block of a function hold good in all the inner blocks it contains; but values can be passed back and forth between independent functions *only* through arguments and returned values, or through external variables, as we'll see shortly. So this program will run:

```
% cat test.c

main()
    {
    int x = 1;
        {
        printf("%d\n", x);
        }
    }
```

```
% cc test.c
% a.out
1
%
```

But not this one:

```
% cat test.c

main( )
   {
   int x = 1;
      {
      inner( );
      }
   }

inner( )
   {
   printf("%d\n", x);      /* line 12 */
   }

% cc test.c
test.c:12: x undefined; func. inner
%
```

We may be belaboring the obvious, but it's a point we have to make. (Users of APL, for instance, might reasonably expect this last example to run.)

    We will say more on the arguments that functions take and the values they return in Chapter 7; the declaration of external variables will be discussed later in this chapter.

### Register Variables

The keyword **register** must be used to define *register variables.* Register variables are one of the ugly parts of the C language. We don't recommend their use; they're confusing and buy you almost nothing. They're used like automatic variables:

```
% cat test.c

main()
   {
   register int x = 1;
      {
      register int x = 2;
         {
         register int x = 3;
         printf("%d\n", x);
         }
      printf("%d\n", x);
      }
   printf("%d\n", x);
   }

% cc test.c
% a.out
3
2
1
%
```

If you are familiar with programming at the assembly-language level, you know that most computers feature internal registers. Registers are "fast"—in other words, operations can be performed upon their contents more quickly than upon data stored in memory. An assembly-language programmer has access to these registers and can move frequently used data into them, thus assuring that his program will run as rapidly as possible. But a programmer using higher-level languages usually doesn't have direct access to his computer's registers. He doesn't know their contents, he doesn't know when any of them are free; but of course the compiler knows, and the designer of C thought it feasible to use the machine's registers to store values that must be manipulated very often during the execution of a program, thus increasing the speed of execution. At least that's the theory. *If* you have specified the storage class of a variable as `register`, and *if* a register is free, and *if* your machine's registers are big enough to hold the variable, then the compiler *may* stick that value in that register. Otherwise the compiler treats `register` variables as it would any other automatic variables—i.e., it stores them in memory.

Experience seems to show that register variables don't really work very well. They complicate the compiler and the language, and on some machines they can't be implemented at all.  So forget them for now.  By the time you know enough to use them, you probably won't want to.

### Static Variables

A declaration that includes *static variables* might look like this:

```
{
static int a;
static int b = 0;
float d = 0.0;
        .

        .

        .

}
```

In this example, the variable d is automatic by default; the keyword static identifies the other variables, whose storage class is static. Apart from that, the declaration of static and automatic variables is identical, always coming at the head of a block.

Like automatic variables, static variables are local to the function (or block) in which they're declared.  The difference is that static variables are not flushed away when the function is finished.  Their values persist; if the program comes back to the same function again it will find that the static variables have the same values they had last time around.  Thus, statics give memory to a function so it can keep count of the number of times an event occurs, fill consecutive elements of an array, etc.

Consider the difference between this example:

```
% cat test.c

main()
    {
    increment();
    increment();
    increment();
    }

increment()
    {
    int x = 0;

    x = x + 1;
    printf("%d\n", x);
    }

% cc test.c
% a.out
1
1
1
%
```

and this one:

```
% cat test.c

main()
    {
    increment();
    increment();
    increment();
    }

increment()
    {
    static int x = 0;

    x = x + 1;
    printf("%d\n", x);
    }
```

```
% cc test.c
% a.out
1
2
3
%
```

Each program calls the function increment three times. increment declares the variable x, which is initialized to zero, and increments its value by 1. In the first example, x is automatic. It is re-initialized to zero each time increment is called; it vanishes when the function terminates and its new value of 1 is lost. The result: x always has the value 1 no matter how many times we call increment.

In the second example, on the other hand, x is static. It is initialized to zero only once; it is never initialized again while the program is being executed. During the first call to increment, x is incremented to 1. This value persists; the next time increment is called, it adds a 1 to x to get a value of 2, and so forth.

We said that initializing the automatic variable x to 1 was just a shorthand for writing

```
{
int x;
x = 1;
   .
   .
   .

}
```

This is *not* true for static variables. The initial value of 1 in the line

```
static int x = 1;
```

is assigned to the static variable x at the time the program is *compiled.* On the other hand, the initial value in the line

```
auto int x = 1;
```

is assigned to the automatic variable x when the compiled program is *run.* The initialization of an automatic variable is what is called a *run-time* phenomenon, whereas the initialization of a static variable is a *compile-time* event; that is, the compiler assigns space in memory for the static variable and stores its initial value there. When the program is actually run, that value is already present.

All this having been said, in general, avoid using static variables unless you really need them. Their values must be kept in memory even when the variables are not active, which means they take up space in memory that could be used by other variables.

Another example of C's friendly defaults: if the programmer doesn't initialize a static variable, the compiler sets its value to zero.* In other words, the example above could have been written more simply this way:

```
% cat test.c

main()
   {
   increment();
   increment();
   increment();
   }

increment()
   {
   static int x;

   x = x + 1;
   printf("%d\n", x);
   }

% cc test.c
% a.out
1
2
3
%
```

## External Variables

*External* variables differ from those we've already discussed in that their scope is *global*, not local. They exist at large, outside any particular function, yet available to any function that wants them. For example:

---

\* By "zero," we mean that if the variable is an int, its initial default value is 0; if a char, '\0'; if a float, 0.0.

```
% cat test.c

int x = 123;                         /* global declaration */

main()
  {
  printf("%d\n", x);
  }


% cc test.c
% a.out
123
%
```

Even though **x** is defined outside **main**, it's accessible inside that function. If there's a conflict of names between global and local variables, the local wins:

```
% cat test.c

int x = 123;                         /* global declaration */

main()
  {
  int x = 321;                       /* local declaration */

  printf("%d\n", x);
  }


% cc test.c
% a.out
321
%
```

There's a logical progression in scope among variables from automatic to static to external. Automatics are local to their own functions (or blocks), and their values are lost when their functions terminate. Statics are local to their functions too, but their values persist—the smile without the cat. Externals are not local to any one function, and their values persist also. They can be handed around from function to function, changing value as the program runs:

```
% cat test.c

int x;                    /* declare external integer x */

main()
   {
   printf("x begins life as %d\n", x);
   addone();
   subone();
   subone();
   addone();
   subone();
   addone();
   addone();
   printf("so x winds up as %d\n", x);
   }

/*
** Increment external integer x.
*/
addone()
   {
   x = x + 1;
   printf("add 1 to make %d\n", x);
   }

/*
** Decrement external integer x.
*/
subone()
   {
   x = x - 1;
   printf("subtract 1 to make %d\n", x);
   }

% cc test.c
% a.out
x begins life as 0
add 1 to make 1
subtract 1 to make 0
subtract 1 to make -1
add 1 to make 0
subtract 1 to make -1
add 1 to make 0
add 1 to make 1
so x winds up as 1
%
```

Notice in this program that the external variable, like static variables, is initialized to zero by default ("x begins life as 0").

Strictly speaking, any function that uses an external variable should declare that variable external via the keyword extern:

```
% cat test.c

int x = 123;

main()
    {
    extern int x;

    printf("%d\n", x);
    }

% cc test.c
% a.out
123
%
```

To summarize, external variables *must* be declared once outside any function, and they *may* be declared again in any function that wants to reference them. The compiler will let you get away without declaring an external inside a function as long as you declare it outside the function *and above it* in the same source code file:

```
% cat test.c

int x = 123;

main()
    {
    printf("%d\n", x);
    }

% cc test.c
% a.out
123
%
```

If you forget to do that, heaven—in the form of the compiler—will help you by telling you that the external is undefined in the function that didn't declare it:

```
% cat test.c

int x = 123;

main()
    {
    printf("%d\n%d\n", x, y,);      /* line 6 */
    }

int y = 321;

% cc test.c
test.c:6: y undefined; func. main
%
```

Most C programmers avoid this problem by declaring *all* their external variables at the top of the source code file, then omitting the extra declarations inside the functions. Of course, if the external variable and the function that references it exist in two separate files, the function must declare the variable anyway. The safest way is of course to declare every external in every function that uses it:

```
% cat test.c

int x = 123;

main()
    {
    extern int x, y;

    printf("%d\n%d\n", x, y);
    }

int y = 321;

% cc test.c
% a.out
123
321
%
```

The safety in this conservative approach has more to do with us than with the compiler. The declarations tell the programmer exactly where all his variables are coming from. That sort of internal documentation is a great help in debugging and updating large programs.

When should you use external variables? The answer is simple: avoid them like the plague. At first glance, and especially to a programmer used to languages that don't allow local declarations, externals seem the answer to a programmer's prayer. All you have to do is declare *all* your variables external and then simply pass them around from function to function as needed instead of using the explicit arguments and returned values described in Chapter 2. In fact the indiscriminate use of externals is an invitation to catastrophe, because in a program that's any size at all you quickly lose track of which variable does what; because the global variables are always there (taking up storage space); because you have lost the advantage of being able to give your variables meaningful local names (i.e., meaningful within the function in which they actually do their work); and because you have lost the advantages of keeping each function an airtight black box.

There's more to learn about storage classes, but this chapter should tell you all you need to know about them for quite a while. Some readers, though, may raise a purely philosphical question: why have storage classes at all? Or rather, why not have just one, so it wouldn't be necessary to specify the one you want?

In practice that's almost the way C works. Automatic variables are king, accounting for the great majority of C declarations. Externals are quite rare (and should probably be rarer). Statics really aren't necessary at all, at least in a theoretical sense. Several very useful subsets of the language make do without them.

But C is a relatively low-level language, used for writing systems code where efficiency is always at a premium. By letting the programmer make fundamental decisions about how his values will be stored and referenced, it gives an important edge to clever coders. No compiler yet written is as smart as a smart programmer, and C cheerfully admits that fact. It doesn't impose its own structure on the programs it's used to create. It doesn't presume to offer some general solution to the problems of data typing and storage. Instead it provides users with the choices they need to solve the problems for themselves, using defaults to urge them gently toward the solutions which are generally thought to be best.

# Chapter 5
# Operators

In this chapter we introduce *operators,* the C language's movers and shakers. C has over 40 different operators, but it's a rare programmer who knows and uses them all. Just as the thousand most common words in English account for the great majority of all words spoken, there are eight C operators that turn up in almost every program. We will concentrate on those for now—the arithmetic operators, the assignment operator, the modulus operator, and the increment and decrement operators—leaving the more specialized ones to later chapters.

### Arithmetic and Assignment Operators

What is an operator? An operator is a symbol which represents some particular operation that can be performed on a data value. The data value itself (which can be either a variable or a constant) is called the *operand.* The operator operates on the operand.

It's much simpler to give examples than to describe. In the expression

    3 + 2 - 1

the symbols + and - are operators and the constants 3, 2 and 1 are operands. Quite simple, really. The operators + and - symbolize the operations of addition and subtraction, of course, and they are used in a C program just as in everyday arithmetic. So the above expression, assuming it's a C expression, tells the compiler to add or subtract these constants. But things aren't really that simple. We have said nothing about the order in which the operations are to be performed or what is to be done with the result.  While we might find the result of a simple expression like this by doing the math mentally and then storing the result (it *is* 4, isn't it?) in our memory in some mysterious fashion, this is not the way a computer works.  A computer must be told explicitly the order in which operations are to be performed and exactly where in its memory the result is to be stored.

Consider the expression

```
a = 1 + 2;
```

which is a complete C statement.  (It is the semicolon that makes it a bonafide C statement.)  The statement has two operators, = and +, and three operands, a, 1 and 2.  The effect of this statement is to add the constants 1 and 2 and assign the result to the variable a, which we will assume has been declared as an int somewhere near the beginning of the program.  As we mentioned in Chapter 3, the = is C's assignment operator.

This tiny example illustrates several important points about the way in which the assignment operator is used in C expressions.  First, it must be understood that the assignment operator of C is not used like the equal sign of algebra.  As we mentioned earlier, we can say

```
a = a + 1;
```

meaning: "Take the current value of a, add 1 to it, and store the result in a again," which is a longish way of saying, "Make a greater by 1," or, "Increment a."  But this C expression is certainly not an acceptable algebraic expression, at least not of the kind that is taught in high school.  On the other hand, high-school algebra permits the expressions

$$1 = 3 - 2$$

$$1 + 2 = 3$$

and

$$a + b = 3$$

none of which is a valid C expression.  The reasons are plain when you think about it.  Having performed some kind of arithmetic operation that produces a value, the computer must find some place in its memory—an addressable location—where it can store this value. A constant doesn't have an address; furthermore, a constant is by definition an unchangeable value. So you can't assign a value to a constant, nor can you change the value of a constant by an assignment. Nor can you assign a value to two variables simultaneously, as you would apparently be doing in an expression like a + b = 3; what would it *mean* to assign a value to something like a + b in the first place? The only possible place where you can store a value is in a variable, which has a name and an address. So the rule is: the value to the left of the assignment operator must *always* be a variable.

The difference between programming practice and algebraic practice is clear enough in these simple cases, but the differences aren't always this obvious. Never take it for granted that the operators in C (even the math operators, which you already know and are comfortable with) behave like their algebraic congeners.

Our a = 1 + 2 example brings out another point regarding C arithmetic. There are two operators in this expression, which means it must be evaluated in two steps: we first add 1 to 2, *then* we assign the result to a. Fine, but how do we know that C will carry out the operations in that exact order? As arithmetic operations become more complicated, we must follow strict rules of *operator precedence* to be sure we write our expressions in such a way as to avoid being surprised by the results. More on operator precedence in C presently.

C has a neat trick of assigning a value to a series of variables in the same statement. It's a kind of domino effect. A simple use of this multiple assignment is shown in the following example where several variables are set equal to the same constant:

```
a = b = c = d = 1 ;
```

A series of assignments like this is always performed one at a time from right to left, so C executes the statement this way:

- assign the constant value 1 to d
- assign the result of the above assignment to c (i.e., assign the value that has just been assigned to d to the operand that is to the left of d—which is c)
- assign the result of the above assignment to b
- assign the result of the above assignment to a

Now how did we *know* that we should evaluate the statement a = b = c = d = 1; from right to left? Well, the only sure way of knowing positively is to refer to a table of associativity and precedence, such as the one below.*

| Operator | Associativity |
|---|---|
| ( )    [ ]    - >    . | left to right |
| !    ~    ++    --    -    *(type)*    *    &    sizeof | right to left |
| *    /    % | left to right |
| +    - | left to right |
| < <    > > | left to right |
| <    < =    >    > = | left to right |
| = =    ! = | left to right |
| & | left to right |
| ^ | left to right |
| ¦ | left to right |
| && | left to right |
| ¦ ¦ | left to right |
| ?    : | right to left |
| =    + =    - =    etc. | right to left |
| , | left to right |

As we said, C has some 40-odd operators and these can affect the evaluation of an expression in subtle and unexpected ways if you aren't careful. Unfortunately, there are no simple rules one can follow, such as the "my dear aunt Sally" mnemonic that tells algebra students they should multiply before dividing before adding before subtracting to ensure they obtain correct results. This is one of C's shortcomings, by the way. You have no single rule, or set of rules, to tell you the precedence of the operators in a complicated expression, or what order to follow when two operators have the same precedence.

Precedence is a problem that every language designer has to face sooner or later. The author of APL, a language with about twice as many operators as C, simply gave up and declared all operators of equal precedence, with right-to-left associativity. That's an easy rule to remember, and as a bonus it greatly simplifies the clockwork of the language. C's designer chose to follow the traditional school of thought which says that certain operators should logically precede others. Alas, the logical necessity of his precedence rules is not self-evident to all

---

* *Associativity* refers to the order in which C evaluates operators having the same precedence. Such operators can associate either right-to-left or left-to-right, as shown in the table. The table itself is based on the table shown on page 49 of Kernighan and Ritchie's *The C Programming Language*, Prentice-Hall, 1978.

programmers. So we must simply refer to the table on page 59 when our memory fails us. This may sound daunting, but when the precedence table's contents are absorbed in small bites, it becomes more palatable. For example, if we concentrate our attention on the order of precedence for the math operators we have been describing, we find it to be

$$
\begin{array}{ll}
(\text{unary minus}) & - \\
& *\quad / \\
& +\quad -
\end{array}
$$

The order of precedence is from top to bottom, with the operators in each row having the same precedence with regard to each other. Thus, the unary minus operator (which negates a value, as in a = -b) has precedence over all the arithmetic operators (in other words, the value of b is first "minus'ed," then assigned to a), and the multiplication and division operators * and / take precedence over the addition and subtraction operators + and - . (Note that the unary - negates its operand's value, while the subtraction operator - is used to subtract one value from another, as in 2 - 1.)

There is a way around the precedence problem and it is a simple one: use parentheses. When in doubt, place parentheses around your operands and operators to make sure the compiler evaluates your expression the way you mean it to be evaluated. The rule for using parentheses is easy. What's inside the innermost pair of parentheses is evaluated first, followed by what's inside the next innermost pair of parens, and so forth. So you can write

```
a = ( b = 1 ) + 2 ;
```

which is quite different from

```
a = b = 1 + 2 ;
```

The first example gives us this sequence of events:

- assign the value of 1 to b
- add the result of the previous operation to 2
- place the result of the previous operation in a

so a contains 3 and b contains 1. The second example gives us this sequence of events:

- add the values 1 and 2
- place the result of the previous operation in b
- place the result of the previous operation in a

so both a and b contain 3.

The helpfulness of parentheses becomes even more apparent when we look at the multiplication and division operators. We know it makes no difference which numbers get added or subtracted first in a long list of additions and subtractions, but it does make a difference with multiplication and division. For example, if we have the expression

```
a = b / c * d;
```

the result we get is very different depending on whether we first divide b by c and then multiply the result by d, or whether we first multiply c times d and then divide the result into b. What we will get in raw C will be the first of these two possible results, since the * and / operators have the same precedence and are associated from left to right. To get the other possible result we have to use parentheses:

```
a = b / (c * d);
```

Double parens and multiple parens are also useful sometimes:

```
a = (b = c / (d * e)) + f;
```

In this example we get the sequence of operations

- multiply d times e
- divide the result of the previous operation into c
- assign the result of the previous operation to b
- add f to the result of the previous operation
- assign the result of the previous operation to a

## The Modulus Operator

The examples we have used so far have all contained integers. What happens in an integer division when there is a remainder? The remainder is simply lost. As far as C is concerned, 5/3 yields 1 and 3/5 yields 0. If you want to know the remainder, you must use the *modulus operator* % , which has the same precedence as the multiplication and division operators:

> (unary minus)  –
>
>        *   /   %
>
>        +   -

The modulus operator is a necessary supplement to the division operator. We use the % like the /, but what we get is the *remainder* instead of the *quotient* of the division:

    5 % 3 yields 2

and

    3 % 5 yields 3

and

    3 % 3 or 6 % 3 or 9 % 3 all yield 0

Get it?  Be careful, though.  The modulus operator will work with int and char values but not with float or double values.

### Mixed Operands and Type Conversion

This raises an interesting point.  What happens if we use mixed operands in an expression—divide a floating-point number by an integer, say, or multiply a char by an int?  Obviously, the result of the operation can have only one type—which does it get?

    When different types are mixed in an arithmetic expression one of the operands undergoes a *type conversion* so it will be in accord with the type of the other operand.  Which one is converted?  The rule is fairly simple.  The primary types we have discussed can be considered to have a kind of rank, or pecking order, like privates, sergeants, and officers in the army, that determines which operand is converted and which is not.  Reading from right to left, the pecking order is as follows:

    char < int < long < float < double

with those on the right outranking those to their left.  Therefore, assuming we are discussing a plain expression that doesn't include an assignment operator,

- if the ranking operand is a `double`, the other operands (regardless of type) are converted to `double` and the result will be a `double`

- otherwise, if the ranking operand is a `float`, the other operands (regardless of type) are converted to `float` and the result will be a `float`

- otherwise, if the ranking operand is a `long`, the other operands (regardless of type) are converted to `long` and the result will be a `long`

- otherwise, all that are left are `int`'s and `char`'s, in which case all the `char`'s are converted to `int`'s and the result will be an `int`

Type conversions can also take place across an assignment operator. Again, the rule is simple. Whatever the type on the right of the assignment symbol, it is converted to the type on the left. If the value on the right has a higher type (as described above), then it will be truncated or rounded to bring it into conformity with the type of the variable on the left of the assignment symbol. In other words, the variable on the left always has precedence.

You can see that the first situation involves *promoting* all the data values in an expression to some highest common denominator, while the second may involve *demoting* the data value that appears to the right of the assignment symbol. It's this demotion that most often causes trouble. Consider what happens in the example on the next page where the library function `printf` prints values at the terminal. (The values that match the *format specification* %c will be printed as characters, those that match the format specification %d will be printed as integers, and those that match the format specification %f will be printed as floats. There is a full discussion of `printf`'s format specifications in Chapter 13.)

```
% cat test.c

/*
** Demonstration of type conversion
** across assignments.
*/
main()
   {
   char c1, c2, c3;
   int i1, i2, i3;
   float f1, f2, f3;

   c1 = 'x';                        /* no conversion */
   c2 = 1000;         /* int constant demoted to char */
   c3 = 6.02e23;      /* float const demoted to char */
   printf("%c %c %c\n", c1, c2, c3);

   i1 = 'x';          /* char constant promoted to int */
   i2 = 1000;                       /* no conversion */
   i3 = 6.02e23;      /* float const demoted to int */
   printf("%d %d %d\n", i1, i2, i3);

   f1 = 'x';          /* char constant promoted to float */
   f2 = 1000;         /* int constant promoted to float */
   f3 = 6.02e23;                    /* no conversion */
   printf("%f %f %f\n", f1, f2, f3);
   }

% cc test.c
% a.out
x h
120 1000 0
120.000000 1000.000000 60200001727189520000000.000000
%
```

When we run the program we get three lines of output. The first line
shows what happens when we assign the constants 'x', 1000, and
6.02e23 to a character variable. As you'd expect, 'x' goes over
unchanged, since it is a character constant. The integer constant 1000
somehow becomes the character 'h', and the floating-point constant
6.02e23 seems to be converted to a nonprinting character since it
doesn't show up in the output.

Converting a float to a char is meaningless, but we can
explain what happened to 1000. Remember that character values are

integers of a limited range, but that range doesn't include 1000 (at least not in the seven-bit ASCII code). The integer 1000 is, therefore, cut short, truncated to a value of 104, which is equivalent to ASCII 'h'. (If you know how numbers are represented in binary notation, you will find the reason for this change easy to grasp. In binary, decimal 1000 is 1111101000 and decimal 104 is 1101000.)

As we see from the next line of output, ASCII 'x' has an integer value of 120. Here the character constant 'x' is promoted when we assign it to an integer variable, and the promotion does it no harm. However, the floating-point constant is demoted rather drastically — from 60200001727189520000000 to zero! Of course the floating-point value is much too large to be represented as an integer (our integers only go up to 32767), and when it's truncated we're left with nothing but zeros.

In the third line everything looks better, since there are no demoted values. True, there's some difference between the representations—'x' doesn't much resemble 120.000000—but nothing has actually been lost, and we could reconvert the floating-point representations back to their original forms. But we certainly weren't batting a thousand overall. If you must mix apples and oranges, be sure you know it. C's invisible type conversions are convenient, but they can give rise to baffling bugs.

### Increment and Decrement Operators

We'll conclude this chapter with a few words on two other much-used C operators, the *increment* and *decrement* operators, ++ and -- respectively. Their places in C's table of operator precedence are as follows:

```
        (unary minus)   -
                      *    /    %
                      +    -
                      ++   --
```

These operators simply add 1 to or subtract 1 from their operand. So the expression

```
    ++a
```

increments a by 1, and the expression

```
    --a
```

decrements a by 1.

These operators can be used either before or after their operand (i.e., in either *prefix* or *postfix* position), so we can have a++ as well as ++a, and a-- as well as --a. Prefix and postfix operators have different effects when used in a C statement. If we assume the value of the variable a to be 5, then execution of the statement

```
b = ++a;
```

will first increase the value of a to 6, and then assign that new value to b. The effect is exactly the same as if the following two statements had been executed:

```
a = a + 1;
b = a;
```

On the other hand, execution of the statement

```
b = a++;
```

will first set the value of b to 5, and *then* increase the value of a to 6. The effect now is the same as if the following two statements had been executed:

```
b = a;
a = a + 1;
```

The decrement operators are used in a similar way, except, of course, the values of a and b are decreased by 1.

# Chapter 6
# Control Structures I

The *control structures* of a computer language enable us to specify which operations are to be carried out by the computer and in what order. That is, the control structures determine the *flow of control* in a program.

In a ponderously written paper succinctly entitled "Flow Diagrams, Turing Machines and Languages with Only Two Formation Rules," C. Böhm and G. Jacopini showed that any algorithm can be coded in a computer language using only three control structures: sequential execution, conditional execution, and looping. Sequential execution is such a common control structure that we seldom think about it; in the absence of any specification to the contrary, it is always the next statement in a sequence of statements that will be executed. The other two control structures, however, need elaboration. In this chapter we'll introduce the `if` and `while`, which are C's simplest equivalents of the B&J formation rules.

### Conditional Execution in C Using the `if`

Conditional execution in its simplest form is specified by the C keyword `if`, which is used like this:

```
if (this condition is true)
    execute this statement;
```

The keyword `if` tells the compiler that what follows, up to the semicolon, is a conditional control structure. The condition itself is

67

always enclosed in a pair of parentheses. If the condition, whatever it is, is true, then the statement is executed. If the condition is *not* true, then the statement is not executed; instead, the program skips past it. This conditionally executable statement may be a single line of code (in which case the semicolon at the end of the line marks the end of the control structure, as above) or it may be a block of code containing several C statements (in which case braces are used to enclose the entire block and it is the closing brace that marks the end of the control structure):

```
if (this condition is true)
    {
    do this;
    and this;
    and this;
    }
```

Note that while a semicolon ends each valid statement within the block there is none after the closing brace. As you may recall from Chapter 2, C statements may be simple statements ending in a semicolon or they may be compound statements consisting of any number of simpler statements enclosed in braces. What we're saying here is that the if-statement may also be a single-line statement ending in a semicolon or a compound statement enclosed in braces.

Here's an example of how the if is used. Suppose we've given a history test to a bunch of students. We'll give all those who score more than 94 an A. The logic of our algorithm can be written as:

```
if (the score is greater than 94)
    the grade is A;
```

(This and the preceding program fragments are written in *pseudo-coding*. Our pseudo-coding follows the rules and style of C but all the statements and conditions are written in plain everyday English. Pseudo-coding is often used to rough out a program and see if it hangs together before the code is actually written. Conversely, if you don't see how someone else's program works, it often helps make things clear if you pseudo-code his program. We shall use pseudo-coding occasionally to explain the logic of our examples.)

Assuming the character variable `grade` will contain the student's letter grade, we can convert our pseudo-coded statement partially into legal C as follows:

```
if (the score is greater than 94)
   grade = 'A';
```

But how do we express the condition itself in C? And how do we evaluate its truth or falsity? As a general rule, we express a condition by using one of C's *relational operators*. The relational operators allow us to compare two values to see whether they're equal to each other, unequal, or whether one is numerically greater than the other. Here's how they look and how they're evaluated by the C compiler:

| *this expression* | *is true if* |
|---|---|
| a == b | a is equal to b |
| a < b | a is less than b |
| a > b | a is greater than b |
| a <= b | a is less than or equal to b |
| a >= b | a is greater than or equal to b |
| a != b | a is not equal to b |

These symbols should be familiar to you except for the exclamation point ! , which is C's symbol for logical negation. So, assuming the integer variable `score` contains the student's test score, we can write this conditional control structure in all-legal C as:

```
if (score > 94)
   grade = 'A';
```

If it is true that the student's score is greater than 94, then give him a grade of A.

Fine, but what if the student gets a lower mark? We can extend the scope of the `if` control structure by including the complementary keyword `else`; the two go together (in pseudo-coding) like this:

```
if (this condition is true)
   execute this statement;
else
   execute this statement;
```

The semicolon at the end of the `else` statement now marks the end of the control structure. If there are several statements in the `else`, they are enclosed in braces, as already described, and the closing brace then marks the end of the control structure.

So now we have two alternatives, and if we had only A students and hopeless dummies in our class, it would be good enough for us to say something like this:

```
if (score > 94)
    grade = 'A';
else
    grade = 'F';
```

In other words, anybody that doesn't get an A fails the course. But that's not realistic and, in fact, it's quite easy to modify the if so that it will handle as many alternatives as you like. Suppose our grading rule is as follows:

| scores | grades |
|--------|--------|
| 95 - 100 | A |
| 85 - 94 | B |
| 70 - 84 | C |
| 60 - 69 | D |
| 0 - 59 | F |

We can code it like this:

```
if (score > 94)
    grade = 'A';
else if (score > 84)
    grade = 'B';
else if (score > 69)
    grade = 'C';
else if (score > 59)
    grade = 'D';
else
    grade = 'F';
```

Note that we use each else-if to select one from among the alternatives. When any of the else-if conditions is satisfied, all the remaining else-if's are skipped. The last else, the one without any condition at all, is a default case—any score not higher than 59 must be an F; there's no need to test it.

If you still find if's, if-else's and else-if's confusing, the diagrams opposite may help. First is a diagrammatic way of looking at an if embedded in a series of sequential statements.

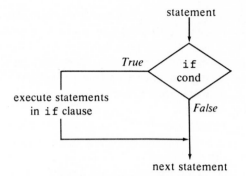

Figure 6.1. An **if** Statement.

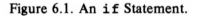

Figure 6.2. An **if-else** Statement.

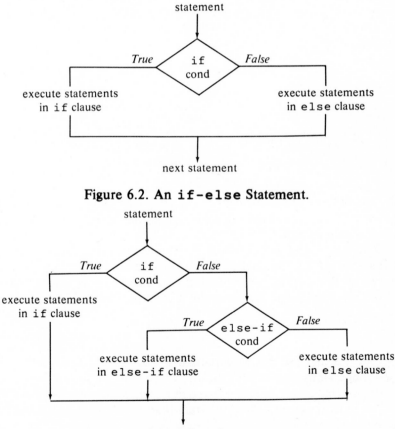

Figure 6.3. An **else-if** Statement.

Now let's add another complication to the example. This test, it seems, was given to a class harboring the notorious student #31670. This 31670 is known to be a sort of idiot-savant. Left to himself he has trouble tying his shoelaces or reading stop signs, but put him in a big classroom and he will always manage to sneak up behind the class brain and copy the brain's answers. So, if old 31670 comes through with an A grade, we're going to flunk him anyway. That's the kind of school *we* run! So we want to add one more condition to this series of `if`-`else`-`if`'s: if the score is over 94 *and* the student's number is 31670, his grade is automatically an F.

We can form logical combinations of conditions, which we can then proceed to test for truth or falsity, by using C's *logical operators*, the `&&` and the `||`. These are single operators, though each is written with two characters. The `&&` is C's *and* operator, the `||` its *or* operator. They are used with C's relative operators in conditional expressions like these:

| *this expression* | *is true if* |
|---|---|
| `a > b && b == c` | a is greater than b *and* b equals c |
| `c != d || d > b` | c is not equal to d *or* d is greater than b |

(Why not use `&` and `|` instead of `&&` and `||`? The single characters are reserved for C's *bitwise* logical operators, which are outside the scope of our primer.)

The *and*'s and *or*'s may be spun out into longer combinations, but it's easy to get confused if you go too far, which is usually a sign that you're not writing your programs as neatly or as cleanly as you might. Still, if we want, we can write a condition like

```
if (a > b || c == d && d < a)
```

If you do go that far, it's important that you know the precedence of these comparisons and combinations. The relational and logical operators are subject to the rules of precedence shown in the table on page 59. The most important thing to remember is that all the relational and equality operators, i.e.

```
>     <     ==     !=     <=     >=
```

take precedence over the logical operators && and ¦¦. In other words, an expression like

    a > b && b == c

is exactly equivalent to

    (a > b) && (b == c)

In expressions where && and ¦¦ are used together, the && takes precedence over the ¦¦. Thus,

    if (a > b ¦¦ c == d && d < a)

is the same as

    if ((a > b) ¦¦ ((c == d) && (d < a)))

which is, after all, much more comprehensible. It's easier to confuse yourself with logical expressions than with arithmetic expressions, so where there are more than a few logical terms involved in a condition—*use parentheses.*

Now that we've absorbed this short lecture, we can take care of the notorious 31670 by adding a new condition to our program:

```
if (score > 94 && student_number == 31670)
    grade = 'F';
else if (score > 94)
    grade = 'A';
else if (score > 84)
    grade = 'B';
else if (score > 69)
    grade = 'C';
else if (score > 59)
    grade = 'D';
else
    grade = 'F';
```

Incidentally, there's no reason why we can't nest one if within another. We could, if we wish, rewrite the above example this round-about way:

```
if (score > 94)
    if (student_number == 31670)
      grade = 'F';
    else
      grade = 'A';
else if (score > 84)
    grade = 'B';
else if (score > 69)
    grade = 'C';
else if (score > 59)
    grade = 'D';
else
    grade = 'F';
```

There is no need to set off the nested if-else with braces since an if-else is considered a single statement in C. The compiler will automatically associate the else with the if that immediately precedes it.

But braces wouldn't hurt; there is no reason why they couldn't be used, like this:

```
if (score > 94)
    {
    if (student_number == 31670)
      grade = 'F';
    else
      grade = 'A';
    }
else if (score > 84)
      .
      .
      .
```

which would help keep a programmer from accidentally misreading the code and associating the wrong if and else. Sometimes with a complicated series of if-else's even the compiler gets addled. Whenever a possible ambiguity exists, *use braces*. For example,

```
if (a > b)
    {
    if (b < c)
      c = a;
    }
else
    c = b;
```

means something quite different from

```
if (a > b)
   {
   if (b < c)
      c = a;
   else
      c = b;
   }
```

If the braces are left out of the first example, it's interpreted by the compiler as if it were the second example, where the compiler attaches the `else` clause to the `if` that immediately precedes it—not the meaning intended in the first example. If you don't see this, perhaps the difference between the two will be more apparent in the following pair of diagrams, in which (a) is the equivalent of our first example and (b) is equivalent to our second:

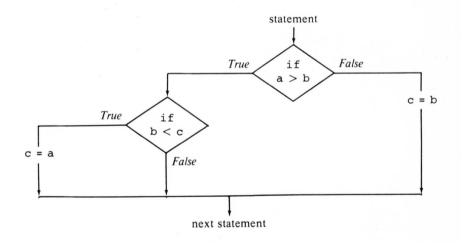

**Figure 6.4(a).**

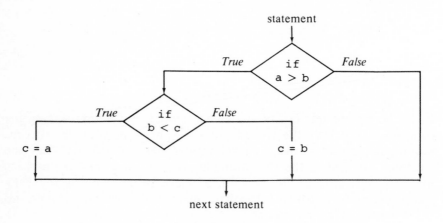

**Figure 6.4(b).**

The crucial difference between the examples lies in the conditions assigned to the else's by the placement of the braces.

### Looping in C Using the while

So much for conditional execution. The other formation rule found necessary by Böhm & Jacopini is looping. In C the fundamental looping construct is the while, which is used like this:

        while (this condition is true)
            execute this statement;

Note how closely this resembles the if construct we have just discussed. The keyword while, the parentheses, and the semicolon are obligatory, just as in the if. The difference is that the while will keep on executing the statement over and over as long as the condition remains true. While the condition is true, the statement is executed. When the statement is, or becomes, untrue, the statement is not executed, and control passes to the first statement that follows the while loop.

The statement controlled by the while may be a single line of code or a block of code containing several C statements. In the latter case, braces are used, as always, to make the statements a single block:

```
while (this condition is true)
    {
    do this;
    and this;
    and this;
    }
```

Note again that there is no semicolon after the closing brace.

The relational and logical operators are used to express conditions for the `while` exactly as for the `if`, and we need say no more about them here. As with `if`'s, one `while` may be nested within another. The compiler, aided perhaps by judiciously placed braces, will keep the `while`'s disconfused.

Here the resemblance between the two control structures ends, for the effect of the `while` is repetitive. Diagramatically, the control structure is handled like this:

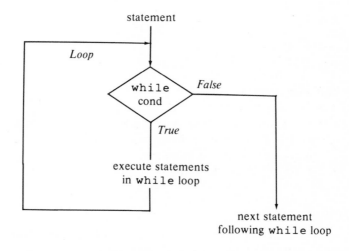

**Figure 6.5.**

Note that if the condition is evaluated and found to be false the first time it is encountered, the statement that follows isn't executed even once. The compiler skips immediately to the first statement following the `while` loop.

As a rule, the `while` must test a condition that will eventually become false, otherwise the loop will circle back forever.* Here is an example of a typical `while` in action:

```
% cat test.c

main ( )
    {
    int i = 0 ;

    while ( i < 5 )
        printf ( "%d\n", i++ ) ;
    printf ( "We're out of the loop.\n" ) ;
    }

% cc test.c
% a.out
0
1
2
3
4
We're out of the loop.
%
```

The sequence of events is as follows:

initialize i to 0;
evalute the condition i < 5;
if this condition is true, execute the first `printf`;
    `printf` prints the current value of i,
    then increments i by one;
    go back and evaluate the condition i < 5 again;

       .

       .

       .

and so on until the condition i < 5 finally tests false;
then print `We're out of the loop.`

We often come upon situations where we want to jump out of a `while` instantly, without waiting to get back to the conditional test.

---

* If a program does begin to loop endlessly, or if it gets away from you for some other reason, don't panic. Every operating system provides some way for you to interrupt a program, usually by pressing a particular key or combination of keys. See your system's user's manual for details.

The keyword **break** allows us to do this. When the keyword **break** is encountered inside any C loop, control passes immediately to the first statement after the loop.

A **break** is usually associated with an **if**. As an example, here is a program that determines whether a number *n* is prime—that is, whether it can be divided by any number except itself or 1 without leaving a remainder. Since these two simple conditions are sufficient to find a prime, a prime-finding program is easy to code. All we have to do to tell whether a number is prime is divide it successively by all numbers from 2 to one less than itself. If the remainder of any of these divisions is zero, the number isn't a prime. How such a program works is shown below in pseudo-coding. We will assume that the value of *n* is set in the program itself, though this is a bit silly, of course. Later we'll see how we can put in any numbers we want while a program's running. Here's the pseudo-coded prime-finder:

```
initialize the counter i to 1;
initialize n to an integer value;

    increment the counter by 1;
    if (counter is equal to or greater than n)
        jump out of this loop;
    if (counter can be divided into n without leaving a remainder)
        print "not prime";
        and jump out of the loop;
    otherwise, continue looping;

we're out of the loop;
if (counter is equal to n)
    we never found a divisor, so
    print "prime";
```

and here is the program in C:

```
% cat test.c

/*
** Test an integer to see if it's a prime number.
*/
main()
  {
  int i = 1;
  int n = 1234;                 /* supposititious prime */


  while (++i < n)
     if (n % i == 0)       /* if n divided evenly by i */
       {
       printf("not prime\n");
       break;
       }
  if (i == n) /* went through loop without break */
     printf("prime\n");
  }


% cc test.c
% a.out
not prime
%
```

See what happens? The `while` loop, using an `if`, calculates n % i for every value of i from 2 to 1234. If the result of any of these calculations is the value 0, in other words if there is no remainder, then n cannot be prime. (This particular program very quickly comes to an end since 1234 divided by 2 is 617, without a remainder.) The program thereupon prints the message `not prime` and `break`s out of the loop, which lands it in the `if` that follows immediately after. Here the i, which is equal to 2 at this point, is compared with n, which is of course equal to 1234. The inequality causes the program to skip to the next statement.

Why does the program require this `if` test at all? Well, there are two ways the program could have gotten out of the loop: (1) it jumped out because n proved not to be a prime, or (2) the loop came to an end because the value of i became equal to the value of n, meaning there was no number between 1 and n−1 that could be divided evenly into n. That is, n is indeed a prime. If this is true, the program should print out the word `prime`.

Note that the `while`'s condition contains the operator `++`. Every time the condition `(++i < n)` is evaluated, the value of `i` increases by 1 before the test is performed. Of course, *something* in a loop has to change or the loop would never end. Moral: don't forget that the test is part of the loop.

Here is a slightly more complex example of a `while` that prints all the prime numbers it finds in the integers from 3 to 32767:

```
% cat test.c
/*
** Find all the primes in the
** integers from 3 through 32767.
*/
main()
    {
    int i;
    int n = 2;

    while (++n <= 32767)      /* n is prime candidate */
        {
        i = 1;
        while (++i < n)
            if (n % i == 0)
                        /* no remainder, n is not prime */
                break;
        if (i == n)
                    /* never divided evenly, n is prime */
            printf("%d\n", n);
        }
    }
% cc test.c
% a.out
3
5
7
11
13
17
19
23
29
 .
 .
 .
```

Here is the program in pseudo-coding:

```
declare the counter i;
initialize n to 2;

    increment n by 1;
    if (n is greater than 32767)
        jump out of this loop;
    set the counter to 1;

        increment the counter by 1;
        if (counter is now equal to or greater than n)
            jump out of this loop;
        if (counter can be divided into n without a remainder)
            jump out of the loop;
        keep on looping;

    we're out of the inner loop;
    if (counter equals n)
        we never found a divisor, so
        print the value of n, which must be prime;
    and keep on looping;
```

This example not only shows how one `while` is nested within another, it also shows that the `break` affects only the `while` of which it is a part—in this case, the inner `while`. Execution of the `break` does not cause an exit from the outer `while`; it only causes the program to jump to the second `if`. So we see that the `break` statement has the effect on a `while` loop shown in Figure 6.6.

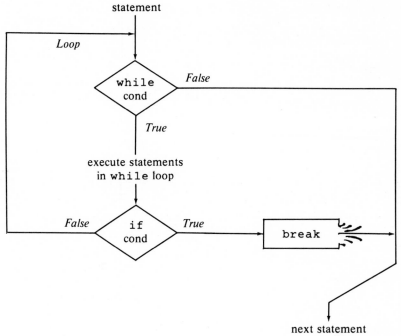

**Figure 6.6.**

But suppose we want the opposite effect instead— *not* to jump out of a loop in order to go to the next statement in the program, but to jump immediately back to the top of the loop again without executing any remaining statements in the block. This is accomplished by using the keyword `continue`, as shown in Figure 6.7. To illustrate the use of `continue`, on pages 84-85 is a small program that prints every number from 1 through 9 except the number 5.

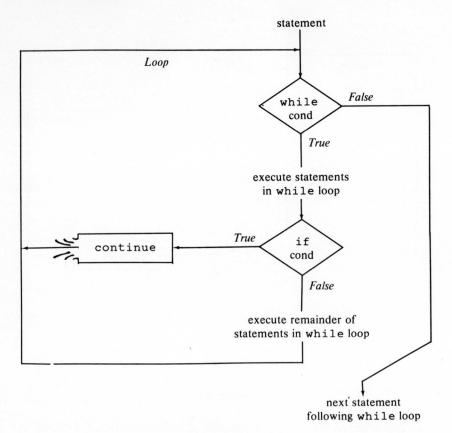

**Figure 6.7.**

```
% cat test.c

main()
    {
    int i = 0;

    while (++i <= 9)
        {
        if (i == 5)
            continue;
        printf("%d\n");
        }
    }
```

```
% cc test.c
% a.out
1
2
3
4
6
7
8
9
%
```

As with the `break`, the `continue` usually works in conjunction with an `if`.

# Chapter 7
# Functions

Now we know enough to be able to write C functions, which means we know enough to write C programs. In this chapter we'll consider how a function is put together and how two or more functions interact with one another.

But first, what is a function in C? It is a self-contained block of code that performs a coherent task of some kind. Think of it as a machine, a "black box" if you like—you put data in and you get data out. The inner workings are invisible, unknowable, to the rest of the program. All the outside world need know about a function are: what goes in; what comes out; what side effects are produced when it runs. Every C program can be thought of as a collection of these black boxes.

There is only one rule about the number of functions in a program and their names: there must be at least one, and at least one must be called `main`. `main` is where program execution begins. Normally, `main` will call other functions, which will in turn call still other functions, and so on.

What do we mean when we say a function "calls" another function? We mean the activity of the function that does the "calling" is suspended temporarily while program control passes to the "called" function. The calling function falls asleep while the called function wakes up and goes to work. When the called function runs out of statements to execute, or when it encounters the keyword `return`, program control returns to the calling function, which comes to life again and begins to execute its code at the exact point where it left off.

Any function can call any other function; it can even call itself. There is in principle no limit to how deeply functions can be nested in this way—main can call function one which calls function two which calls function three which . . . and so on ad infinitum.  Nor are there any predetermined relationships, rules of precedence, or hierarchies among the functions that make up a complete program.  Except for what we have said about main starting things off, C functions enjoy a state of perfect equality.  One function can call another function it has already called but has in the meantime left temporarily in order to call a third function which will sometime later call the function that has called it, if you see what we mean.  No?  Well, let's give a few simple examples of different calling sequences.

To begin at the very beginning, how exactly does one function call another?  By naming it.  Here's an example:

```
% cat test.c

main()
    {
    printf("I'm in main.\n");
    }

% cc test.c
% a.out
I'm in main.
%
```

main is only one line long.  This single line of code, however, is a *function call*—that is, it names another function, printf, to which program control is immediately transferred.  How do we know that

```
    printf("I'm in main.\n");
```

is a function call?  Because there are a pair of parentheses attached to printf(...), which in this case happen to enclose the character string, "I'm in main.\n".  (The parentheses after a function name need not necessarily enclose anything at all, but the parentheses must always be there nevertheless; that's how the C compiler recognizes a function call.)  The function printf is not defined in our example program but of course it has to be defined somewhere.  This somewhere is the collection of standard library functions that comes with every C compiler—see Chapter 13.

Increasing the complexity of our program a bit, we can have main call several functions:

```
% cat test.c

main()
   {
   printf("I'm in main.\n");
   alaska();
   bermuda();
   california();
   }

alaska()
   {
   printf("Now I'm in alaska.\n");
   }

bermuda()
   {
   printf("Now I'm in bermuda.\n");
   }

california()
   {
   printf("Now I'm in california.\n");
   }

% cc test.c
% a.out
I'm in main.
Now I'm in alaska.
Now I'm in bermuda.
Now I'm in california.
%
```

Increasing the complexity of our program another notch, here is an example of nested function calls:

```
% cat test.c

main()
   {
   printf("I'm in main.\n");
   alaska();
   printf("I'm finally back in main.\n");
   }

alaska()
   {
   printf("Now I'm in alaska.\n");
   bermuda();
   printf("Here I am back in alaska.\n");
   }

bermuda()
   {
   printf("Now I'm in bermuda.\n");
   california();
   printf("Back in bermuda.\n");
   }

california()
   {
   printf("And now I'm in california.\n");
   }

% cc test.c
% a.out
I'm in main.
Now I'm in alaska.
Now I'm in bermuda.
And now I'm in california.
Back in bermuda.
Here I am back in alaska.
I'm finally back in main.
%
```

Take the time to trace through the way in which program control is transferred among these functions. Since main is the first function called, every other function in a given C program is called either directly or indirectly by main. That is, main *drives* the other functions. Programs are often written this way. main is designed to call a list of other functions or it executes a loop which drives the rest of the program. In the chapters that follow, we'll show you many examples of how main acts as a driver, either to make an entire program perform some desired action or to test a newly written function, to make sure the function does what it's supposed to do.

Don't be afraid to write functions which are called only once. Don't try to squeeze an entire program into main; this is considered very bad style. Instead, try and break a program up into small units—functions—that correspond to its logical subdivisions.

Here is a more elegant example of how functions can be nested. This time we will use another library function, putchar, in place of printf. (We've already met putchar in Chapter 2; it simply prints one character.)

```
main()
  {
  r();
  }

a()
  {
  putchar('a');
  d();
  putchar('a');
  }

d()
  {
  putchar('d');
  }

r()
  {
  putchar('r');
  a();
  putchar('r');
  }
```

What happens when we run this program? Right! Good for you! Seek and ye shall find!

As we mentioned, it is quite possible for a function to call itself:

```
% cat test.c
main()
    {
    printf("Here we are in main\n");
    main();
    }
% cc test.c
% a.out
Here we are in main.
Here we are in main.
Here we are in main.
Here we are in main.
Here we are in main.
Here we are in main.
Here we are in main.
Here we are in ^C*
%
```

A function that calls itself this way is an example of *recursion*, which is used fairly often in C. We won't pursue recursion any further now because it usually involves pointers and arrays, neither of which we have discussed yet.

Well, maybe we could pursue it just a little bit. How about a simple program that makes use of recursion to compute factorials? We can use this program to illustrate how arguments are passed from one function to another, and how the values calculated by a called function are returned to the calling function. For those of you out there in humanities-land without the vaguest notion of what factorials are, the factorial value of a number *n* is expressed in math symbology as *n!* (called "n factorial"), and it means there is a series of repetitive multiplications, starting with $n \times n-1$, with each result being multiplied the next time around by a number that is one less in value than the multiplier in the preceding multiplication. So five factorial (5!) is $5 \times 4 \times 3 \times 2 \times 1$ is 120. OK? Here's the program itself:

---

* We stopped the listing on our system by typing a "control-c" at our terminal. Your operating system may have a different way of interrupting an executing program.

```
% cat test.c

main()
   {
   int i = 0;

   while (++i < 6)
      printf("%d! is %d\n", i, factorial(i));
   }

/*
** Return n!.
*/
factorial(n)
int n;
   {
   if (n == 1)
      return(1);
   else
      return(n * factorial(n-1));
   }

% cc test.c
% a.out
1! is 1
2! is 2
3! is 6
4! is 24
5! is 120
%
```

Now let's see how the program works. Here first is a pseudo-coded version:

```
main:
```

    declare the counter i and initialize it to zero;
    increment the counter;
    `while` (counter's value is less than 6)
        call `factorial` with counter value as actual argument;
        print value of counter and
          value returned by `factorial`;
        increment the counter again;

```
factorial:
```

> if (argument received has a value of 1)
>    return value of 1;
> else
>    multiply the argument by value of
>      factorial of the argument − 1;
>    return calculated value;

Program execution begins at main, of course. We declare the variable i as an int and give it an initial value of zero. Then we simply go around the while loop, setting the value of i to 1, 2, 3, 4, and 5 at successive iterations. At each iteration we print the value of i and of i factorial, using the function factorial to compute the factorial value.

More explicitly, whenever main reaches the statement

```
printf("%d! is %d\n", i, factorial(i));
```

the expression within the parentheses is evaluated (C always evaluates what's inside the innermost parentheses first), which means in this case that the function factorial is called before the function printf. And what happens in factorial? The first time it's called, factorial discovers that the value of its argument, shown as i in the calling function and as n in the called function (we'll clarify the difference in a moment), is equal to 1. So the condition test (n == 1) succeeds, causing factorial to return control to main, along with the value 1, as indicated in the line

```
return(1);
```

Back in main, the function printf is called. It prints the line:

```
1! is 1
```

Simple enough. Now let's go into greater detail.

### Arguments and Returned Values

Simply put, an argument is a data value that you want to pass from one function to another. You identify the data value as an argument by enclosing it in parentheses after a function name. We have already discussed arguments briefly in Chapter 2, mainly to get the nomenclature

decrements a by 1. straight. Let's review. There are two kinds of arguments in C functions, actual and formal. When one function calls another, the argument specified in the function call is an *actual* argument. In our program, in the line

```
printf("%d! is %d\n", i, factorial(i));
```

the i of the function call `factorial(i)` is an actual argument. On the other hand, the argument enclosed within the parentheses of the function being called is a *formal* argument. Thus, the n in the function name `factorial(n)` is a formal argument.

In this program, the first time we go around the `while` loop in `main`, the variable i is first incremented, then tested for its equality to the constant 6. If i is less than 6, then the line

```
printf("%d! is %d\n", i, factorial(i));
```

is executed, and the program passes the current value of i to `factorial`. That is, the value of the actual argument, which is 1, is copied over `factorial`'s formal argument, n; i.e., n also takes the value 1. Program execution now jumps to `factorial`. The condition ( n == 1 ) is tested and found to be true, which means the next line

```
return(1);
```

returns the value 1 to `main`.

As far as `main` is concerned, what seems to have happened is that its original function call in its entirety has been replaced by the value 1. In slow motion, the transformations by which this replacement occurs are as follows. The original statement

```
printf("%d! is %d\n", i, factorial(i));
```

turns out to be exactly equivalent to

```
printf("%d! is %d\n", 1, factorial(1));
```

which in turn is exactly equivalent to

```
printf("%d! is %d\n", 1, 1);
```

which is why `main` prints

    1! is 1

On the second pass through `main`'s `while` loop, i is set to 2. This time when the line

    printf("%d! is %d\n", i, factorial(i));

is executed, `main` transfers control to `factorial` together with an actual argument value of 2. That is, the value of n in `factorial` becomes 2. Now the ( n == 1 ) test in `factorial` fails, so we go on to the statement

    return(n * factorial(--n));

And here is where we meet recursion.

How do we handle the expression ( n * factorial(n-1) )? We see we must multiply n by `factorial(n-1)`. Since the current value of n is 2, it's the same thing as saying that we must return the value ( 2 * factorial(1) ). We know that the value of `factorial(1)` is 1, so the expression reduces to ( 2 * 1 ), or simply 2. Thus, the return statement

    return(n * factorial(n-1));

passes the value 2 back to `main`, which duly prints

    2! is 2

Perhaps now you can see what happens as the value of i is incremented from 1 to 2 to 3 to 4 to 5. `main` calls `factorial` with its actual argument and waits for `factorial` to send back a computed value. Before doing so, `factorial` calls `factorial` and waits for a value to be returned; but it's possible for the `factorial` it calls to call yet another `factorial`, the argument being decreased by 1 for each of these recursive calls.

We speak of these successive calls to `factorial` as being different *invocations* of `factorial`. These successive invocations of the same function are possible because the C compiler keeps track of which invocation calls which. Internally, it's as if the compiler assigned identifying tags to each invoked `factorial` to avoid confusing them, and to keep their argument values separated.  The recursion ends finally when the last invocation gets an argument value of 1, which the preceding invocation of `factorial` now uses to calculate *its* own returned value; and so back up the ladder again.  So we might say that what happens is

*factorial(5) returns (5 times*
    *factorial (4), which returns (4 times*
        *factorial(3), which returns (3 times*
            *factorial(2), which returns (2 times*
                *factorial(1), which returns (1)))))*

which is the same thing as

    *factorial(5) returns (5 times*
                *4 times*
                *3 times*
                *2 times*
                *1)*

which is, all in all, a pretty good definition of a factorial.  Moral: recursion may seem strange and complicated at first, but it's often the most direct way to code an algorithm—and, once you are familiar with recursion, the clearest way of doing so.

But what about all the different values of n?  Don't they get confused?  No, because each invocation of `factorial` gets its own copy of the argument.  As always in C, the values of variables local to the calling function are held in suspension while those of the called function are active, even when the functions in question are two copies of the same thing.

### Arguments and Black Boxes

It may be that our explanation has been too complicated, so much so that the essence of argument-passing has eluded you.  If so, it might help make things clearer if we review what we have just said, this time ignoring what goes on in particular functions.  Remember that what goes on in any given function is unknown to any other function.  That is, every function is a black box to every other function.  These black boxes can communicate or cooperate with one another only via their arguments, their returned values, or their side effects.  It follows that if we want to describe the purpose of any particular function, we need know only three things about it: (1) what arguments does it require (i.e., what are its inputs?); (2) what result does it return (i.e., what is its output?); and (3) what side effects does it have (i.e., how does it affect things outside itself?).

It's important to understand that the called function cannot alter the actual arguments in the calling function. That is, what we have been describing with our black-box functions is a scheme in which we pass the *value* of the actual argument. The variables themselves are not handed over to the called function. When the compiler encounters a function call in a program, it makes a *copy* of the arguments in the function call; it is these copies that are passed along to the called function. Since only copies of values are being manipulated, the original values in the calling function aren't affected at all by what happens inside the called function. The calling and called functions thus communicate across a barrier designed to prevent accidental contamination.

Of course, the type of the actual argument in the calling function should match the type of the formal argument in the called function. In our example, the actual argument i must be an int because the function `factorial` declares n as an int. Some harmless type conversions are carried out by the compiler—actual arguments of type char are always promoted to int's when they are passed to a function, and float's become double's—but don't take chances: *make* arguments match.

## More on Data Types

We have one last topic to consider in this chapter, the declaring of a *function*'s data type. Let's consider an example using a function that simply squares its argument and then returns the squared result. C has no intrinsic or primitive operator that raises numbers to a given power, so a function to perform such operations is occasionally necessary. Here's a program that prints the square of 2, the square of that square, and so forth up to 256:

```
% cat test.c

main()
    {
    int i = 2;

    while (i < 256)
        printf("%d\n", i = square(i));
    }

/*
** Square the integer x.
*/
square(x)
int x;
    {
    return(x * x);
    }

% cc test.c
% a.out
4
16
256
%
```

By now you should have no problem understanding how a program such as this works. But consider the variation on the opposite page. What happened? We were expecting the series 2.25, 5.0625, etc.— certainly not negative squares.

The answer is that the function **square** was designed to square integers, not floating-point values. The internal conversions, deconversions, and reconversions confused things hopelessly. What can we do about this situation? We'll have to write another version of **square** that squares float's and double's:

```
/*
** Square a float or double.
*/
double xsquare(x)
double x;        /* line 15 */
    {
    return(x * x);
    }
```

```
% cat test.c

main( )
   {
   float i = 1.5;

   while (i < 256.0)
      printf("%f\n", i = square(i));    /* NO! */
   }

/*
** Square the integer x.
*/
square(x)
int x;
   {
   return(x * x);
   }
% cc test.c
% a.out
-28672.000000
1024.000000
%
```

---

Notice that in this new definition, which we've named xsquare to avoid confusion, the argument x is declared as a double in the function header. We have also declared the function itself as a double. Why did we do that? To make sure the function square returns a value having the type double. So we've specified *both* the type of the argument and the type of the returned value in this function definition. (We didn't have to declare the type of the returned value in our original version of square because C assumes that any undeclared function type is an int. And since char's are converted to int's when they are passed to or returned from a function, int also works for char's.)

OK. Now let's have another go at our program with our newly created xsquare. We should get perfect results this time, shouldn't we?

```
% cat test.c

main( )
   {
   float i = 1.5;

   while (i < 256.0)
      printf("%f\n", i = xsquare(i));
   }

/*
** Square a float or a double.
*/
double xsquare(x)
double x;          /* line 15 */
   {
   return(x * x);
   }

% cc test.c
test.c:15: xsquare redeclared
%
```

What went wrong? Well, we forgot to tell you—whenever you have a called function that is not of type `int` (that is, if it returns a value that is other than an `int` or a `char`), you must declare that function in every function that calls it.* The declaration of the called in the calling function must always look like this:

   *type name-of-called-function* ( ) ;

where *type* is the data type returned, *name-of-called-function* is the name of the function, and ( ) ; is invariant—it must always be there. So we must modify our program to declare the function `xsquare` in `main`:

---

* To confuse the issue further, if the definition of the called function appears *above* the definition of the calling function in the same source code file, you can omit the declaration. The situation is really the same as that described for the declaration of external variables in Chapter 3; function definitions are considered external data objects. Avoid confusion by declaring *all* non-`int` functions in the functions that call them.

```
% cat test.c

main( )
   {
   float i = 1.5;
   double xsquare( );

   while (i < 256.0)
      printf("%f\n", i = xsquare(i));
   }

/*
** Square a float or a double.
*/
double xsquare(x)
double x;
   {
   return(x * x);
   }

% cc test.c
% a.out
2.250000
5.062500
25.628906
656.840836
%
```

It is true that C programmers seldom use double's or float's but there are many functions that return values having derived types— in fact, it's cases like those that account for most of the type-specification required in connection with functions.

Of course, it doesn't *hurt* to declare the type of every function when you write it, or to declare every function in every other function that calls it. If nothing else, such thoroughness is good documentation. And it's also very good for the soul, we're sure.

# Chapter 8
# The C Preprocessor

Unless this book sells big in Novaya Zembla and Ulaan Goom, our readers should be familiar with *string replacement* from some of the junk mail they get:

> *Dear Mr. Potrzebie:*
>
> *Have you ever thought what the world would be like without pelagic ooze? As President of the Society to Limit Underwater Damage from Geothermal Exploitation, I'm making a personal appeal to you and the whole Potrzebie family . . .*

It doesn't take a very suspicious turn of mind to guess that the original of that letter exists in a more general form:

> *Dear TITLE SURNAME:*
>
> *Have you ever thought what the world would be like without pelagic ooze? As President of the Society to Limit Underwater Damage from Geothermal Exploitation, I'm making a personal appeal to you and the whole SURNAME family. . .*

Or, more likely still:

> *Dear TITLE SURNAME:*
>
> *Have you ever thought what the world would be like without CAUSE? As OFFICER of the ORGANIZATION, I'm making a personal appeal to you and the whole SURNAME family . . .*

At some point between conception and mailing, all occurrences of the string *TITLE* are replaced by *Mr.*, all occurrences of the string *SUR-NAME* are replaced by *Potrzebie*, and presto, Mr. Potrzebie gets a "personalized" letter from S.L.U.D.G.E. You can see the usefulness of string replacement in writing form letters, especially in the second version, which can be used by almost any send-us-your-money society.

String replacement has great value in programming, too. For one thing, it's a way to give constants meaningful names. For example, in a program that makes use of Avogadro's constant, 6.0247E23, it makes good sense to use the name AVOGADRO instead of 6.0247E23 throughout the code, then arrange somehow to replace all instances of AVOGADRO by 6.0247E23 when the program is compiled. String replacement of this kind greatly increases the generality of your program. It also makes updates easier. A financial program that uses the prime interest rate as a constant might have to be recompiled fairly often to keep up with fluctuations in that rate, in which case it would certainly be wise to use a name like PRIME_RATE throughout the source code for whatever value the prime rate happens to be. There should be just one place in the program where we can set the name PRIME_RATE to the correct value whenever a change is necessary, instead of combing through every line of the code for every occurrence of the prime rate.

Perhaps most important of all, string replacement of this kind can make a program portable. Suppose we are writing a C program that reads data from a magnetic tape. We want the machine to stop reading the tape when it encounters a certain marker value. Our computer installation uses the number −1 as this end-of-tape marker, but your computer installation uses something else. The program will work for us but not for you. But if we change the end-of-tape value −1 to the name EOT throughout the source code, *we* can make use of the program simply by defining EOT to mean −1 while *you* can make use of the same program by defining EOT to mean whatever value your installation has adopted. All you need do is define EOT to this value, recompile the source code, and the program will run on your machine.

These conveniences have been worked into C, but not as a part of the language *per se*. String replacement is a facility of the C *macro preprocessor*, which is part of the complete C package, along with the library routines. The preprocessor is just what its name implies: it's a program that processes your source code *before* it passes through the compiler, replacing certain names (like AVOGADRO or EOT) with their defined equivalent strings. You can certainly write C programs without knowing anything about the preprocessor or its facilities, but it's such a great convenience that virtually all C programmers rely on it. In this chapter we'll discuss its most often used features: *simple string replacement*, *macro expansion* and *file inclusion*.

### Simple String Replacement

Here is an example of simple string replacement. The following function uses the radius of a circle to compute and return its area:

```
double area(radius)
double radius;
  {
  return(3.1415926536 * radius * radius);
  }
```

Now let's write a *macro definition* in which the value 3.1415926536 is identified with the name PI:

```
#define PI 3.1415926536
```

Macro definitions such as this are usually placed at the head of a program, but in any case before the first use of the macro in the code. Having written the definition, we can thereafter write PI in the source code wherever we mean 3.1415926536:

```
#define PI 3.1415926536
     .
     .
     .
double area(radius)
double radius;
  {
  return(PI * radius * radius);
  }
```

These two versions of the function are exactly equivalent.

What could be simpler than this kind of string replacement? We write a macro having the general form

```
#define string1 string2
```

when we want the preprocessor to replace every occurence of *string1* in the source code by *string2*. The #define appears just that way, and *string1* is separated from both #define and *string2* by one or more blanks or tabs. (And note that the definition is *not* terminated by a semicolon, as we would expect it to be if it were C code.)

The entire command line is called a *macro definition*. The name of the macro is *string1* and the replacement string is *string2*. More formally, *string1* is called the *macro template* and *string2* is the *macro expansion*. In our example PI is the template, and 3.1415926536 is the expansion. Notice that PI is in capital letters. It's a tradition in C programming to use all-caps for the names of constants defined by macros, and to keep other names in lower case. This makes it easy for programmers to pick out defined constants when reading through a program.

Once the macro definition has been written, every instance of PI within the body of the source code is in effect a *macro call*. Before the source code goes through the compiler it is examined by the preprocessor for any macro definitions. If there are any, the preprocessor searches through the source code for the corresponding macro calls. Wherever it finds one, it replaces the macro name with the appropriate replacement string. Only after this procedure has been completed is the program handed over to the compiler. Thus we see, assuming we use an editor to create the original source code, that our program must pass through five different processors before it is ready to be executed:

|  |  |
|---|---|
| editor | *input* from terminal; |
| | *output* is a source code file containing C source code and (maybe) preprocessor commands |
| preprocessor | *input* is source code file; |
| | *output* is source code file with macros expanded and other files included as indicated by preprocessor commands |
| compiler | *input* is source code file with macros expanded, etc.; |
| | *output* is assembly language source code |
| assembler | *input* is assembly-language source code file; |
| | *output* is relocatable object code |
| linker | *input* is relocatable object code modules from your programs and from C library; |
| | *output* is executable code (i.e., a.out) |

In most systems, the preprocessor, assembler and linker are invoked automatically when the compiler is used. (Go back to Chapter 1 if you want to review the details of the compilation process.)

It's an excellent idea to use the preprocessor's #define feature for *all* constants that appear in your programs. A constant's value may have to be changed some day; it's nice to know that you can change all instances of it all at once, and without exception, by rewriting a single #define. This doesn't matter much for small programs like the ones shown in this primer, but large projects can run into thousands of lines of code, and a constant may appear very many times.

The macro preprocessor will *not* expand macro names placed inside quotation marks. Compare what happens in this program

```
% cat test.c

#define HELLO "bonjour\n"

main()
  {
  printf(HELLO);
  }

% cc test.c
% a.out
bonjour
%
```

with what happens in this one:

```
% cat test.c

# define HELLO bonjour

main()
  {
  printf("HELLO\n");
  }

% cc test.c
% a.out
HELLO
%
```

Once a name has been #define'd in one macro, it can be used as part of the macro expansion in a subsequent #define. So

```
#define PI  3.1415926536
#define PISQUARE  PI*PI
```

is perfectly legal.

## Macros With Arguments

The preprocessor also allows you to write string-replacement macros having arguments. Suppose we have a fairly big program that needs to figure out the area of different size circles at different times. We've already seen that we can write a function which takes a circle's radius as an argument and spits out the area as a returned value. We can do something similar with a macro. All we need do is write the macro definition with the desired arguments:

```
#define  area(x) (3.1415926536 * x * x)
```

As in a function definition, the **x** in this macro definition is a formal argument. (You will recall having met formal and actual arguments in the last chapter.) What happens now is this. The preprocessor scans the source code. Every time it finds the four characters "**area**" followed by an actual argument inside parentheses (which makes the macro call look just like a function call), it replaces the macro name with its macro expansion, at the same time replacing the formal argument with the actual argument. As an example, suppose we write the following source code:

```
% cat test.c

#define area(x)  (3.1415926536 * x * x)

main()
   {
   printf("%f\n", area(2.5));
   }

%
```

After this code has passed through the preprocessor, what the compiler gets to work on will be this:

```
main()
    {
    printf("%f\n", 3.1415926536 * 2.5 * 2.5);
    }
```

How do we know?  We can see what the preprocessor does by compiling the program with the E-switch set.  This is a UNIX convention that causes the preprocessor to run by itself.  Instead of sending the preprocessed source code on to the compiler, it sends it to our terminal:

```
% cc -E test.c
# 1 "test.c"

main()
    {
    printf("%f\n", (3.141596536 * 2.5 * 2.5));
    }
%
```

(The # 1 "test.c" simply identifies the source code file.)
    There are two points of syntax you should keep in mind when writing #define's that have arguments.  First, note that in the macro definition

```
#define area(x) (3.141596536 * x * x)
```

we've been careful to leave no space between area and (x); second, note that the entire macro expansion (3.141596536 * x * x) is enclosed by parentheses.  The first point is essential.  If we were to write area (x) instead of area(x), the (x) would become part of the macro expansion, which we certainly don't want.  What would happen would be this.  We write

```
% cat test.c

#define area (x) (3.1415926536 * x * x)   /* bad! */

main()
    {
    printf("%f\n", area(2.5));
    }
%
```

and we get

```
% cc -E test.c
# 1 "test.c"

main()
   {
   printf("%f\n", (2.5) (3.1415926536 * 2.5 * 2.5));
   }
%
```

which won't run.  Not at all what we wanted.

Our point about using parentheses is just that it's a good safety measure.  Since we can't always forsee the environment any macro will be expanded into, it's wise to encapsulate the expansion by enclosing it in parens.  Here's an example of what could happen if we fail to enclose a macro expansion within parentheses.  The following function correctly divides 27 by the square of 3:

```
% cat test.c

#define square(n) (n * n)

main()
   {
   printf("%f\n", 27.0/square(3.0));
   }

% cc test.c
% a.out
3.000000
%
```

But this version of the function doesn't work so well:

```
% cat test.c

#define square(n) n * n                 /* watch out */

main()
   {
   printf("%f\n", 27.0/square(3.0));
   }
```

```
% cc test.c
% a.out
27.000000
%
```

What went wrong? If we compile this function with the **E**-switch set, we can see the macro was expanded this way:

```
% cc -E test.c
# 1 "test.c"

main()
    {
    printf("%f\n", 27.0/3.0 * 3.0);
    }
%
```

Remember that / and * associate left-to-right, which means the arithmetic was performed this way:

( 27/3 ) * 3 yields 9 * 3 yields 27

Though macro calls are "something like" function calls—they certainly look the same in the source code and in most cases produce the same results—they are not really the same thing. This is as important to remember as it is easy to forget. Consider the following pair of examples. The first is a simple function call:

```
% cat test.c

/*
** Print squares of integers from 1 to 10.
*/
main()
    {
    int i = 1;

    while(i <= 10)
        printf("%d\n", square(i++));
    }

square(n)
int n;
    {
    return(n * n);
    }
```

```
% cc test.c
% a.out
1
4
9
16
25
36
49
64
81
100
%
```

No mysteries there.  Here is the same program written with a macro in place of the function square:

```
% cat test.c

#define square(n) (n * n)

/*
** Print squares of integers from 1 to 10.
*/
main()
    {
    int i = 1;

    while(i <= 10)
        printf("%d\n", square(i++));
    }

% cc test.c
% a.out
1
9
25
49
81
%
```

Obviously something went wrong.  The E-switch shows us what:

```
% cc -E test.c
# 1 "test.c"

/*
** Print squares of integers from 1 to 10.
*/
main()
  {
  int i = 1;

  while(i <= 10)
    printf("%d\n", (i++ * i++));
  }
%
```

The preprocessor did its job all right: it replaced the formal argument n by the actual argument i++, and with disastrous results.  The problem is that every instance of the macro call

```
square(i++)
```

was replaced by the macro expansion

```
(i++ * i++)
```

because the replacement string was defined as

```
(n * n)
```

Always remember that *the C preprocessor doesn't know C.*  It replaces one string with another in a stupid, unthinking, literal way, and that's *all* it does.  We happen to be using the preprocessor to simplify our C source code, but it could just as well be used to expand strings in a Fortran or Basic program—or to write form letters to Mr. Potrzebie. Moral: however much alike they look, a macro call is *not* a function call.  Use upper case macro names to avoid confusion.

Which brings us to the question: when is it best to use macros with arguments and when is it better to use a function?  In general, macros make a program run faster while function calls make it smaller. If you use a macro a hundred times, the macro expansion goes into your source code in a hundred different places.  On the other hand, whether you use a function a hundred times or just once, it will always take up the same amount of room in your compiled program.  But passing arguments and getting back a returned value does take a little doing, and may slow your program down, especially if the function is called a hundred times (inside a loop, for example). So, if the macro is brief, just a simple expression like the ones in our examples, it makes a nice shorthand and avoids the overhead associated with function calls. On the other hand, if you have a fairly large macro and it's used fairly often, perhaps it ought to be a function.

## File Inclusion

The third preprocessor feature we want to discuss is file inclusion. The preprocessor command line for file inclusion looks like this:

    #include "*filename*"

and it simply causes the entire contents of *filename* (which must have the double quote marks around it as shown) to be inserted into the source code at that point in the program. Of course this presumes the file exists and is available by the rules of your operating system.

When and why is this feature used? If you have a very large program, the code is best divided into several different files, each containing a set of related functions. There are several reasons for doing this. Perhaps there is a limit on how large a file your operating system or editor can handle; in any case, it's good programming practice to keep different phases of a large program separate and to compile them separately. The files can be linked together later.

Each of these separate files can begin with an #include "*filename*" which pulls in a file of definitions that establish the values to be used throughout the entire program. For example, you may decide to use the following constants in all your source code files:

```
#define BUFSIZ 128
#define EOL '$'
#define FALSE 0
#define NEWLINE '\n'
#define NO 0
#define NULL '\0'
#define PAGELEN 66
#define TAB '\t'
#define TRUE 1
#define YES 1
```

Once these definitions have been decided upon, they can be stored in an include file called something like `defs.h`. (The `h`, for "header," is conventional but not mandatory.) Thereafter, every source-code file would begin with the control line

```
#include "defs.h"
```

which would make these macro definitions available to the program.

The `#include` command line can take another form:

```
#include <filename>
```

without the quotes. The difference is that `#include` *<filename>* looks for *filename* in a prearranged list of directories outside your own directory while `#include` *"filename"* (with the quotes) searches both your directory and the prearranged list. For example, some C installations require you to begin your source code files with the command line

```
#include <stdio.h>
```

meaning "standard input/output," if you intend to use the standard input/output functions described in Chapter 13. This is because the standard functions and macros are available in the system header file, `stdio.h`.

The preprocessor can do other tricks as well—you can undefine a defined string, you can compile certain lines of code conditionally (depending on the value of a certain expression at the time of compilation), you can alter the line count, and you can even rename the source code file internally. But these exotic features are seldom used and not within the scope of this primer.

# Chapter 9
# Arrays

Computers process data. Quite often the data are organized in some orderly manner—a statistical time series, for example, or the output of an experiment that varies as the input is varied, or a list of names in alphabetic order. A collection of data whose elements form an ordered sequence is called an *array*. The elements of an array can be of any data type (as long as they are all the same type), so we can have an array of int's, an array of double's, an array of char's, etc., even an array of arrays, since, in fact, the array is one of C's secondary data types, that is, it can be derived from a primary data type. This is another example of the way in which C habitually makes use of its simpler elements to build more complex structures.

In this chapter we shall discuss the characteristics of C arrays and the notation in which they are described. In the next chapter we shall discuss how the elements of an array can be manipulated through the use of pointers.

## Array Definitions

Suppose we have a collection of anything in sequence—say a row of rooms in a small motel:

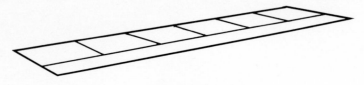

**Figure 9.1.**

Now suppose we count the number of people in each room:

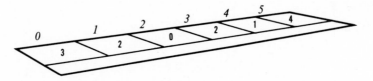

**Figure 9.2.**

Starting from room 0 (because C always begins a count from an origin of zero) we get these values:

$$
\begin{array}{c}
\text{room } 0 - 3 \text{ occupants} \\
"\quad 1 - 2 \quad " \\
"\quad 2 - 0 \quad " \\
"\quad 3 - 2 \quad " \\
"\quad 4 - 1 \quad " \\
"\quad 5 - 4 \quad "
\end{array}
$$

A single row of values like this is usually called a *linear array*.

Suppose we have a somewhat larger motel with two rows of rooms:

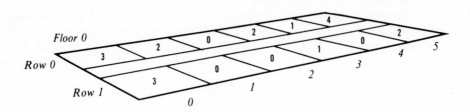

**Figure 9.3.**

We might now organize the rows and the rooms in each row in this order:

```
row 0, room 0 — 3 occupants
 "   0,   "   1 — 2      "
 "   0,   "   2 — 0      "
 "   0,   "   3 — 2      "
 "   0,   "   4 — 1      "
 "   0,   "   5 — 4      "

row 1, room 0 — 3 occupants
 "   1,   "   1 — 0      "
 "   1,   "   2 — 0      "
 "   1,   "   3 — 1      "
 "   1,   "   4 — 0      "
 "   1,   "   5 — 2      "
```

This is an example of an *array of arrays*, or a *two-dimensional* array, or (if you prefer) a *matrix*. There are two elements (rows), each of which contains six sub-elements (rooms).

An even larger motel might have two floors, each floor with two rows of six rooms each:

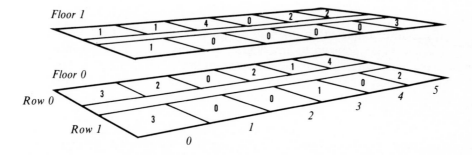

**Figure 9.4**

So now we have three dimensions, and we need three numbers to identify each room:

```
floor 0, row 0, room 0 — 3 occupants
  "   0,  "  0,   "    1 — 2      "
  "   0,  "  0,   "    2 — 0      "
  "   0,  "  0,   "    3 — 2      "
  "   0,  "  0,   "    4 — 1      "
  "   0,  "  0,   "    5 — 4      "

floor 0, row 1, room 0 — 3 occupants
  "   0,  "  1,   "    1 — 0      "
  "   0,  "  1,   "    2 — 0      "
  "   0,  "  1,   "    3 — 1      "
  "   0,  "  1,   "    4 — 0      "
  "   0,  "  1,   "    5 — 2      "

floor 1, row 0, room 0 — 1 occupants
  "   1,  "  0,   "    1 — 1      "
  "   1,  "  0,   "    2 — 4      "
  "   1,  "  0,   "    3 — 0      "
  "   1,  "  0,   "    4 — 2      "
  "   1,  "  0,   "    5 — 2      "

floor 1, row 1, room 0 — 1 occupants
  "   1,  "  1,   "    1 — 0      "
  "   1,  "  1,   "    2 — 0      "
  "   1,  "  1,   "    3 — 0      "
  "   1,  "  1,   "    4 — 0      "
  "   1,  "  1,   "    5 — 3      "
```

This is an example of an *array of arrays of arrays*. You can see how the idea can be generalized to any degree of complexity, though you'll have to visualize what a four-dimensional motel might look like yourself, since we don't know how to draw it. Though impossible to visualize, arrays with up to five dimensions are perfectly acceptable in our reference compiler.

How does C deal with arrays? This is actually a two-part question: First, how does the C notation indicate arrays and the operations performed on arrays? Second, how are C arrays represented internally within a computer?

## Array Notation

To begin with, an array must be declared. We declare an array just as we would any other data object, but we add square brackets [ ] after its name, usually with a number inside that indicates the number of elements in the array. For instance, to declare a linear array of six integers, the array being named a, we write

```
int a[6];
```

To declare a linear array of 130 floating-point numbers, the array being named b, we write

```
float b[130];
```

Once an array is declared, how do we reference any given element? By enclosing a *subscript* within a pair of square brackets that follow the name of the array; the subscript indicates which element of the array we are referencing. Subscripts may be any integer constant or variable, or any expression which returns an integer. Here, for example, is how we assign the value 1 to the third element in the array a:

```
a[2] = 1;
```

Wait, didn't we say the *third* element? Yes, but the subscript's [2]. How can that be? Well, as we said, C always begins counting array elements from 0, not from 1. That is to say, the array begins with a zeroth element, a[0], instead of a[1]. We agree with what you're thinking: it's annoying that an array declared as int a[6] should not contain the element a[6] (its highest element is a[5]), but there's a reason for beginning a count with zero, which will become evident when we get into pointers; for now you must just accept the fact.

Here's a program that shows how we declare an array that contains the data of our simplest motel example, then adds up the elements of the array to get the total number of guests:

```
% cat test.c

main()
   {
   int room[6], i, total;

   room[0] = 3;
   room[1] = 2;
   room[2] = 0;
   room[3] = 2;
   room[4] = 1;
   room[5] = 4;
   total = 0;
   i = 0;
   while (i < 6)
      total = total + room[i++];
   printf("Total occupancy: %d\n", total);
   }

% cc test.c
% a.out
Total occupancy: 12
%
```

Of course this example's unrealistic—no one would assign values permanently inside a function just to add them up—but you get the idea. Note that we can declare room on the same line as i and total, since the elements of room are int's.

### Internal Representation of Arrays

How does C handle the values in such an array internally? Well, it's something like the organization of the motel itself: C stores the values in sequential locations. In other words, the compiler reserves six adjacent int locations in the computer's memory, then fills them with the appropriate values, like this:

base location + 0 → room[0] contains the value 3
base location + 1 → room[1] contains the value 2
base location + 2 → room[2] contains the value 0
base location + 3 → room[3] contains the value 2
base location + 4 → room[4] contains the value 1
base location + 5 → room[5] contains the value 4

This amount of detail may seem excessive, but in fact it's very important, since knowing how the elements of an array are stored in memory is the key to using pointers with arrays. More on that in the next chapter; the astute reader will have guessed already how C pointers work.

In Chapter 3, when we discussed simple data types, we showed how they are initialized. C arrays can be initialized also, but *only* when their storage class is either `extern` or `static`; no initialization of `automatic` arrays is permitted. Initialization looks like this for a linear array:

```
static int room[6] = {3, 2, 0, 2, 1, 4};
```

The compiler goes from left to right, matching each value inside the braces with each element of the array. So `room[0]` is initially assigned the value of 3, `room[1]` is assigned the value 2, and so on. A handy variation is:

```
static int room[] = {3, 2, 0, 2, 1, 4};
```

In this case the compiler will count the number of items within the braces for you and then define an array having that many elements, so the explicit declaration, `room[6]`, isn't really necessary. Of course, this shortcut works only when you initialize all the elements in an array, as in this example.

Incidentally, C does not provide what's called *dynamic allocation* of array space.* In some languages you can specify the size of an array as a variable such as `size`, then feed in the values of `size` when you actually run the program. Never in C. In C you must specify the size of the array explicitly when you declare it. On the other hand, when the same array is redeclared elsewhere in the program you need not be so explicit. (Functions that expect arrays as arguments would have very little generality if you always had to specify the size of the array— you'd need a different function for an array having 5 elements, another for an array having 6 elements, and so on.) For example, if a function called `addum` were written to add the elements of an integer array of known size, its declaration might look like this:

---

* More precisely, the C language *per se* has no such capability. Most versions of C offer a library function that does dynamic storage allocation.

```
addum(array, size)
int array[], size;
    {
    int sum = 0;

    while (--size >= 0)
        sum = sum + array[size];
    return(sum);
    }
```

The function's first argument is an array, but because we're presuming it's been declared elsewhere in the program we don't have to indicate how big it is when we declare the array as an argument in addum. Nor do we have to specify the size of an array in a function if the array is externally defined. Here for example is a program in which main simply adds up the numbers from one to ten contained in an array, with the array itself defined outside of main:

```
% cat test.c

int array[] = {1, 2, 3, 4, 5, 6, 7, 8, 9, 10};
int size = 10;

main()
    {
    int sum = 0;

    while (--size >= 0)
        sum = sum + array[size];
    printf("sum is %d\n", sum);
    }

% cc test.c
% a.out
sum is 55
%
```

## Multidimensional Arrays

How about those multidimensional arrays that make us feel like Gödel E. Bach when we figure out a use for them?  C treats an array of arrays just as the name implies, so that if, for example, we declare a two-dimensional array named **x**, each dimension of which contains six integers, we declare it as

```
int x[2][6];
```

To reference an individual element in this array of arrays we also need two sets of brackets.  For instance, the statement

```
x[1][2] = 1;
```

assigns the value 1 to the second element of the first array in the two-dimensional matrix **x**.  If that's too abstract, think of our motel with its two rows of six rooms each.  If we declare an array:

```
int rooms[2][6];
```

we can assign number-of-occupant values thus:

```
rooms[0][0] = 3; /* row 0, room 0 has 3 guests */
rooms[0][1] = 2; /* row 0, room 1 has 2 guests */
        .                       .
        .                       .
        .                       .
rooms[1][4] = 0; /* row 1, room 4 has 0 guests */
rooms[1][5] = 2; /* row 1, room 5 has 2 guests */
```

and the values in this matrix would be stored internally thus:

base location + 0 $\rightarrow$ row 0, room 0 contains the value 3
base location + 1 $\rightarrow$ row 0, room 1 contains the value 2
            .                  .
            .                  .
            .                  .
base location + 10 $\rightarrow$ row 1, room 4 contains the value 0
base location + 11 $\rightarrow$ row 1, room 5 contains the value 2

And how do we initialize such an array?  Would you believe:

```
static int [2][6] = {{3, 2, 0, 2, 1, 0},{3, 0, 0, 1, 0, 2}};
```

or, if that looks too complicated:

```
static int [2][6] = { {3, 2, 0, 2, 1, 0},
                      {3, 0, 0, 1, 0, 2}};
```

The second initialization is identical to the first, but it shows more clearly how the values in the matrix are arranged. If you read the constant values from left to right (3, 2, 0, etc.) and row by row you are reading them in the order in which they are stored in the computer's memory.

Incidentally, the way in which the values are stored guarantees that the rightmost subscript of a pair or set will vary most often. In other words, the values are stored beginning with rooms[0][0] followed immediately by rooms[0][1], and so on, not by rooms[1][0].

## String Arrays

One more thing before we go on to pointers. There's a special kind of array that is used very much in C and this is a good place to introduce it. It's called a *string*. A string is a one-dimensional array of ASCII characters terminated by a null. A string can be represented in C by enclosing its characters (sans null) inside *double* quotation marks. For example:

```
"This is a string!"
```

is a string. More exactly, it's an array with 18 elements—count 'em. Do you count only 17? Ah, but you forgot the null! C inserts the null automatically, so really we have this array:

| | | |
|---|---|---|
| zeroth element | — | 'T' |
| first element | — | 'h' |
| second element | — | 'i' |
| third element | — | 's' |
| . | | |
| . | | |
| . | | |
| fifteenth element | — | 'g' |
| sixteenth element | — | '!' |
| seventeenth element | — | '\0' |

Note that the null character '\0' is quite a different thing from the ASCII zero '0'. The null is expressed in binary notation as 00000000, while the ASCII '0' is expressed in binary as 00110000.

Note also the distinction between, for example, 'T' and "T".

The ′T′ represents the letter T while the "T" represents a string made up of two characters, ′T′ and ′\0′. It follows that there is no such thing as a completely empty string; even the expression "" represents a string with one element—the null character.

A string is a kind of constant in C, so it can be used to initialize a variable, as long as the variable is a character array. Here is a simple example:

```
% cat test.c

char string[] = "This is a string!";

main()
   {
   int i = 0;

   while (string[i] != '\0')
      {
      printf("%c = %d\n", string[i], string[i]);
      ++i;
      }
   }

% cc test.c
% a.out
T = 84
h = 104
i = 105
s = 115
  = 32
i = 105
s = 115
  = 32
a = 97
  = 32
s = 115
t = 116
r = 114
i = 105
n = 110
g = 103
! = 33
%
```

The compiler prints the decimal equivalent of every ASCII value in the string, except the final '\0'. Incidentally, we can have `printf` print the whole string simply by using the format specification %s:

```
% cat test.c

char string[] = "This is a string!";

main()
    {
    printf("%s\n", string);
    }

% cc test.c
% a.out
This is a string!
%
```

`printf` knows it must stop when it gets to the null that marks the end of the string.

This should be enough on arrays for the present. We'll be discussing them further, and strings especially, in the chapters that follow.

# Chapter 10
# Pointers

One thing that sets C apart from similar structured languages is its extensive use of pointers. To a considerable degree it is C's use of pointers that makes it the excellent systems language that it is. And what is a C pointer? It is a variable that, unlike other C variables, doesn't contain a data value; instead, it *points to* a variable that does contain a data value. Examples should make clear what a C pointer is and what it does.

Let's begin with a variable we will call var1. Like all the other C variables we have described so far, var1 is a name that stands for a data value of some type: a char, an int, a float, etc. We should appreciate by now that the names we assign to the variables in our source programs are both arbitrary and entirely for our own convenience. The names help *us* remember what is happening in our programs. The computer, if it could think, would no doubt be amused by this evidence of our human frailty. It, of course, "thinks" exclusively in terms of numbers and never forgets a single one of them.

When a source program is compiled, all the variable names in the program are transformed into the addresses of memory locations, and the appropriate data values are loaded into these locations. The names are then thrown away. When the program is executed, it is entirely in terms of these memory locations and the data values stored therein.

The point we are making is that the variable names we use in our source programs are nothing more than stand-ins for specific memory locations, locations that are assigned when the program is compiled and linked. Furthermore, when we write an assignment statement such as

```
var2 = var1;
```

what happens when the program is executed is that the data value contained in location `var1` is copied into the location assigned to `var2`. In other words, the *value* represented by the variable name on the right-hand side of the assignment operator is copied into the *location* assigned to the variable name on the left-hand side of the operator.

### Pointer Operations

Now to describe the pointer notation used in C. The operator & is placed before a variable name to indicate that we want the *address* of that variable, not its current value. For example, the expression `&var1` means "the address of `var1`," not the data value that `var1` happens to contain. Therefore, an assignment statement like

```
ptr = &var1;
```

means "take the *address* of `var1` and save it in the variable named `ptr`." `ptr` is called a *pointer variable*, i.e., it holds (or "points to") the address of another variable.

What does this assignment accomplish? Since `var1` holds a data value—let's call it *x*—what we have done is make *x* available to the program by way of the pointer variable `ptr`, since `ptr` now *also* holds *x*'s address.

In C, the operator * refers to the *contents* of the memory location being pointed to by whatever variable name follows the *. For example, `*ptr` might be translated into bookish English as "that which is contained at the location specified by `ptr`."

Since the & refers to the address of a variable, it is called the *address-of* operator. Its friend * is known as the *indirection* operator, since it provides indirect access to a value. Once `ptr` has been set to point to an address, we can get at the contents of that address by using the * operator. For example, the statement

```
var2 = *ptr;
```

can be understood to mean: "assign the value located at the address being pointed to by `ptr` to the variable `var2`." So the two assignment statements

```
ptr = &var1;
var2 = *ptr;
```

perform exactly the same function that is performed by the single assignment statement

```
var2 = var1;
```

Is that all? Why go to all this bother simply to transfer a value? Perhaps the following analogy will help show what it is that a pointer does. Suppose there is a young man who has an apartment. He has the only key and, therefore, he is the only person who has access to the apartment and its contents. Suppose this young man has a friend who stays with him for a while and to whom he gives a copy of the doorkey. In C notation, this event can be described as:

```
friend = &owner;   /* friend gets address of owner */
```

Now the friend also has access to the apartment and its contents.

Unknown to the owner of the apartment, his friend has a girlfriend to whom he cannot resist presenting gifts, even when these gifts belong to the apartment's owner. The result can be described by:

```
friend = &owner;  /* friend gets address of owner */
girl = *friend;  /* girl gets everything owner has */
```

which is not exactly the same thing as the direct assignment:

```
girl = owner;
```

though the end result is the same.

In this little story the friend acts like a C pointer, that is, he is an intermediary who effects the transfer of the contents of the apartment to a third party without the first party's knowledge or consent. But what is the advantage of being able to transfer a data value indirectly via a pointer rather than directly from one variable to another? In this simple case, none. But in more complicated cases, as when dealing with the elements of an array or structure (as we shall describe), pointers are very useful.

Remember that when we are writing a program we don't know what addresses will be assigned to the variables we are using. Addresses are assigned to variables only when a program is compiled.

Since we can't know what the address of a variable will be, it is difficult for us to do many extremely useful things, such as manipulating the values in an array. C's pointer notation allows us to specify machine addresses symbolically, that is, to pretend that we *do* know where particular data values are located so that we can reach into these locations and manipulate their contents directly, just as can be done in assembly language programming. If you are familiar with assemblers, the advantages of pointers should be apparent to you. If you aren't, take our word for it that pointers can help make a program clear, succinct, and efficient.

Some teachers of computer science are down on C's pointers. They say the pointers are too "powerful," that when they are used indiscriminately they can screw up a program royally and undo all the good done by following the rules of structured programming. This is certainly true but it is also, we think, a narrow view. You don't *have* to use pointers if you don't want to; you can achieve the same results in other ways, though with greater difficulty; but pointers are one of the glories of C and they do make for elegantly written programs. If you do use pointers, treat them with as much respect as you would a fast car, which is no more dangerous than a slow one in getting from A to B, unless you drive it carelessly. And a good programmer, like a good driver, should never be careless.

### Pointer Declarations

Now that we've introduced pointers, here's a simple program that shows how they are actually used. This program does nothing more than print the letter **X**:

```
% cat test.c
main()
  {
  char lettera, *letterb, letterc;

  lettera = 'X';
  letterb = &lettera;
  letterc = *letterb;
  printf("%c\n", letterc);
  }

% cc test.c
% a.out
X
%
```

After our lengthy introduction to pointers, how the character constant
'X' is transferred from one variable to another, finally to be printed
by printf, should be obvious to you. If not, here is a pseudo-coded
outline of the program:

> declare character variables lettera, letterc;
> declare character pointer letterb;
>
> assign the character constant 'X' to lettera;
> assign the address of lettera to pointer letterb;
> assign the value being pointed to by letterb to letterc;
> print the value assigned to letterc;

We are already familiar with declarations like char lettera
and char letterc, which tell the compiler to set aside locations in
memory for two variables, each of which will contain a character value.
But what about the declaration char *letterb? This declaration
tells us that the memory location set aside for letterb will contain a
*pointer* to a character value, or, to be more precise, that the expression
*letterb will return a character value.

When this program is compiled, the character constant 'X' is
first assigned to the memory location associated with the variable
lettera. When the compiled program is run and the statement

```
letterb = &lettera;
```

is executed, the address of lettera is assigned to the memory location associated with letterb. Finally, when the statement

```
letterc = *letterb;
```

is executed, the value in the address being pointed to by letterb is
assigned to the memory location associated with letterc.

If you still don't understand how pointers work, perhaps the following diagrams will help dispel any confusion. When this program is
compiled, the declarations cause three cells in memory to be reserved
for the variables lettera, *letterb, and letterc (Figure
10.1). These cells have addresses, of course. Although we can't really
know what address each of these variables will have, let's assume
they're as follows:

`lettera` is assigned location 1000
`letterb` is assigned location 1100
`letterc` is assigned location 1200

We can think of these locations as mailboxes with the occupant's name and address stenciled on each of them. Though the illustrations show the mailboxes are the same size, they're not really. Their size will depend on their contents, since in our reference computer pointers require more space than characters.

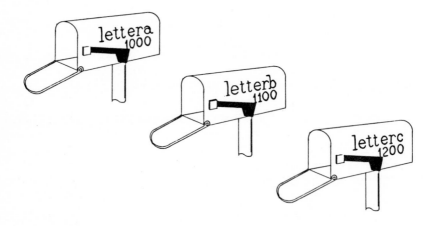

**Figure 10.1.**

Now the assignment

`lettera = 'X'`

causes someone (the postman, presumably) to put the character value `'X'` into `lettera`'s box (Figure 10.2). And the assignment

`letterb = &lettera`

tells the same postman to put the address of `lettera` (in other words, 1000) into `letterb`'s mailbox (Figure 10.3). The last assignment

`letterc = *letterb`

**Figure 10.2.**

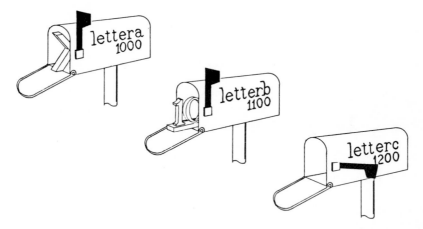

**Figure 10.3.**

says in effect, "Go to `letterb`'s mailbox and remove its contents. You will find that these contents are an address. Put a *copy* of what you find at that address into `letterc`'s mailbox." When the postman carries out these instructions, what we wind up with is shown in Figure 10.4, on the next page.

## Pointers as Function Arguments

This example has been too simple, and therefore somewhat artificial,

**Figure 10.4.**

for there's seldom any reason to use a pointer merely to point to a single variable. It's in more complex situations that pointers let you streamline your code, and especially when you're dealing with arrays or structures or, as in the next example, with function arguments. Both of the examples that follow make a function call and pass an argument, but one passes its argument as a pointer.

In Chapter 7 we described how argument values are passed from a calling function to a called function, not by passing the actual values but by passing copies of them. This *call-by-value* technique keeps you from accidentally changing the values in the calling function. But suppose you *want* to change them; what then? Suppose you want to change lower-case ASCII letters to upper-case. One way of doing so is to write a function—let's call it 1tou, "ell-to-you"—that gets a character value as its argument, shifts that character value to upper case if it's a lower-case letter, and returns that new value to the calling function. The function 1tou is shown on the opposite page.

Let's walk through this program, both to review what we've already said about argument passing and also because the program contains several points of programming interest.

The function main calls two other functions, the library function putchar (which prints a single character at the terminal) and the user-supplied function 1tou. Because it's inside the parentheses that enclose putchar's arguments, 1tou is called first. It takes an argument of its own, and we can see from its function definition that the

```
% cat test.c

/*
** Print the upper-case equivalent of
** the character constant 'x'.
*/
main()
   {
   putchar(ltou('x'));
   putchar('\n');                       /* newline */
   }

/*
** Given an ASCII character, return
** its upper-case equivalent.
*/
ltou(c)
char c;
   {
   if (c <= 'z' && c >= 'a')       /* it's lower case */
     return(c + 'A' - 'a');              /* upper it */
   else
     return(c);              /* it's already upper case */
   }

% cc test.c
% a.out
X
%
```

---

argument it's expecting is a single char value. main passes it the character constant 'x'. ltou's job is to return the upper-case equivalent.

In ltou, the passed argument is checked to see if has an ASCII value between 'a' and 'z':

```
if (c <= 'z' && c >= 'a')
```

This if statement includes an operator we described briefly in Chapter 5, the logical AND operator, &&. The if statement is true only if *both* c <= 'z' *and* c >= 'a' are true. If either c <= 'z' or c >= 'a' is *not* true, then the entire statement is false. Since in this case the if statement is true, the return statement

```
return (c + 'A' - 'a');
```

is executed, which returns the character value `'X'` to `main`. If the `if` statement were not true, `c` would be returned unchanged.

The `if` statement says in effect, "If `c` is a lower-case letter (i.e., if its value falls between `'a'` and `'z'` in the table of ASCII values) then return `c` plus the constant that makes the difference between upper- and lower-case letters." Now, in ASCII the letters `'A'`, `'a'` and `'z'` have numeric values of 65, 97, and 122, respectively, so we could have written the `if` statement in our program this way:

```
if (c <= 122 && c >= 97)
    return(c + 65 - 97);
```

or just

```
if (c <= 122 && c >= 97)
    return(c - 32);
```

the `32` being the numerical difference between upper- and lower-case ASCII letters. But all these numbers look rather mysterious, whereas

```
if ( c <= 'z' && c >= 'a')
    return(c + 'A' - 'a');
```

states pretty clearly what it is we're trying to do. (States it clearly in human terms, of course. To the C compiler, the two versions would be exactly equivalent.) Incidentally, since both `'A'` and `'a'` are constant values, the subtraction `'A'` - `'a'` will be done when the program is compiled and will not be repeated when the program is executed—in other words, it doesn't slow things down to write `'A'` - `'a'` rather than `32`.

The numeric value of the ASCII `'x'` is 120, so the logic of `ltou` handles it this way:

Is 120 less than or equal to 122?
    Yes.
Is it also greater than or equal to 97?
    Yes.
Then return the value (120 − 32), which is of course 88.

And 88 is the numeric value of ASCII `'X'`.

So we see that the value returned by `ltou` to `main` is `'X'`,

and, therefore, main calls putchar with the argument 'X', and
this is why it's 'X' that appears at our terminal. The second call to
putchar simply prints a newline; in other words, it causes the print
head to return to the left margin and begin a new line.

### Passing Arguments as Pointers

Now let's make a subtle change in ltou by using a pointer argument:

```
% cat test.c

/*
** Replace the value of a character variable
** by its upper-case equivalent.
*/
main()
    {
    char c = 'x';

    ltou(&c);
    putchar(c);
    putchar('\n');                              /* newline */
    }

/*
** Given a pointer to a character variable,
** change its value to the upper-case equivalent.
*/
ltou(cptr)
char *cptr;
    {
    if (*cptr <= 'z' && *cptr >= 'a')
        *cptr = *cptr + 'A' - 'a';
    }

% cc test.c
% a.out
X
%
```

Things don't look too different. We start off in main with the
variable c being declared a char and assigned the character constant
'x'. Immediately after, there is a function call:

```
ltou(&c);
```

whose argument this time is the *address* of **c**. OK, let's see what happens in our new version of **ltou**.

The formal argument of **ltou** is **cptr**, which is declared to be a pointer variable of type **char**. That is to say, the value contained in the address that **cptr** is pointing to is a **char**.

The **if** statement looks very like the **if** statement in our first version of **ltou**, but this time we are dealing in pointer values. The program checks to see whether the value *cptr (i.e., the value being pointed to by **cptr**) is a lower-case ASCII character. 'x' is a lower-case letter, of course, so the statement

```
*cptr = *cptr + 'A' - 'a';
```

is executed. It is this statement that changes the actual character value in **main** from 'x' to 'X'. As before, ASCII 'A' is decimal 65, ASCII 'a' is decimal 97, and the value of the character in the address being pointed to (the ASCII 'x') is, we know, decimal 120. When we perform the required calculation, $120 + 65 - 97$, the result is 88, the same as before. This value is assigned to *cptr. Since **cptr** is pointing to the value in **main** named **c**, assigning the ASCII value 88 to *cptr means assigning the same value to **c** in **main**. So we've found a way around the safety device that prevents a called function from changing the values of the actual arguments in a calling function.

In a way this seems like cheating, and perhaps it is. However, we can plead two excuses:

- The notation used to call a function with a pointer argument is clearly different from that used to call a function that has non-pointer arguments, so we're not likely to do it by accident.
- Use of pointers enables us to get around the limitation that C functions can return only a single value. As we'll see in a few pages, pointers make it easy to deal with an array of values as well as with a single value.

Let's summarize what happened in our last program:

- The character constant 'x' is assigned to the variable **c**.
- The function **ltou** is called with the passed argument being the *address* of **c**.

- Because `cptr` is the address of `c`, `*cptr` provides indirect access to `c`'s contents.
- `ltou` examines the contents of `c`, via `*cptr`, checking whether they are a lower-case ASCII character value.
- The value is indeed lower-case so the equivalent upper-case value is calculated and placed, via `*cptr`, into `c`.
- Control is then returned to `main`, which prints out `'X'`.

## Pointers and Arrays

We have said that pointers are rarely used with simple data objects like individual `char`'s and `int`'s. The only complex data type we've considered so far is the array and, in fact, arrays and pointers are intimately connected. C guarantees that the elements in an array will occupy contiguous addresses in memory and this makes it possible for us to think of an array as consisting of a base address—which is the beginning element of the array—plus an offset value for each subsequent element in the array, the value of each offset depending on the distance of its element from the base address. For the zeroth element of the array, the offset is zero; for the first element, 1, and so forth. For example, suppose we have the string `"That's all, folks!"`. As we mentioned in the last chapter, a string is a one-dimensional character array, so we can use it to initialize an external or static array of type `char`:

```
static char byebye[] = "That's all, folks!";
```

which declares `byebye` as an array whose elements are the following ASCII characters:

```
byebye[0]    'T'
byebye[1]    'h'
byebye[2]    'a'
byebye[3]    't'
       .
       .
       .
byebye[16]   's'
byebye[17]   '!'
byebye[18]   '\0'
```

(Remember, by definition every string ends with the null character `'\0'`.)

The base, or starting, address of `byebye` is the address of its zeroth element, 'T'. Its first element, 'h', is located at base address+1, its second element, 'a', is at base address+2, and its final element, the null '\0', is at base address+18. That's the way the C compiler handles arrays internally. When, for example, you ask what's in byebye[16], it adds 16 to the base address of byebye and looks at that location to see what's there.

But that's really working with pointers, isn't it? If we set a pointer to the base address of an array, we can find the address of any element in that array by adding the correct offset value to that pointer. In fact, C provides facilities that allow us to perform a limited amount of *pointer arithmetic*. We can:

- Initialize a pointer to the address of a given data object, or to zero.
- Increment or decrement a pointer.
- Add an integer to a pointer.
- Subtract an integer from a pointer.
- Compare two pointers (using operators like == and !=, etc.).
- Subtract one pointer from another, provided both pointers point to objects of the same type.

When we do pointer arithmetic, C takes into account the fact that different types of data objects occupy different amounts of memory. If, for example, charptr is declared to be a char pointer, then charptr+2 will point to an address two characters above charptr. But if dblptr is declared as a double pointer, then dblptr+2 will point to an address that is two *double-precision* values above dblptr. That's quite a difference—in our reference compiler each double fills enough memory to hold four char's. C does this kind of scaling automatically so you don't have to worry about it.

Now about that relationship between pointers and arrays. . . Consider the program on the opposite page. You understand how the program works, don't you? We'll explain it anyhow.

We begin by declaring the static array byebye and initializing it to the string "That's all, folks!" (Remember, we can't initialize automatic arrays.) Then we declare the pointer charptr local to main and initialize it to point to the 18th element of byebye—i.e., to the null byte at the end of the string.

On the first go-around in the while loop, we decrement the pointer so that it points to the next lower element of the array (that is, to the 17th element of byebye), and we check whether the element

```
% cat test.c

/*
** Print the string <byebye> backwards.
*/
main()
    {
    static char byebye[] = "That's all, folks!";
    char *charptr = &byebye[18];

    while (--charptr >= &byebye[0])
        putchar(*charptr);
    putchar('\n');
    }

% cc test.c
% a.out
!sklof ,lla s'tahT
%
```

---

now being pointed to is greater than or equal to the zeroth element of
byebye. It isn't, so we print the character being pointed at and then
we go around the while loop again. The result, naturally enough, is
that the string is printed in reverse.

Note that we wrote the loop as

```
while (--charptr >= &byebye[0])
```

An experienced C programmer would probably write this expression as

```
while (--charptr >= byebye)
```

There's a simple rule that explains why he would do so: *the name of an
array stands for the address of its zeroth element, that is, for its base
address.* So

```
&byebye[0]
```

and

```
byebye
```

mean the same thing, assuming `byebye` has been declared as an array.

Another C convention is that a string expressed as "*string*" is in fact a pointer to the zeroth character of "*string*". This means we can rewrite the function in a simpler way:

```
% cat test.c

/*
** Print the string "That's all, folks!" backwards.
*/
main()
  {
  char *ptr1, *ptr2;

  ptr1 = "That's all, folks!";
  ptr2 = ptr1 + 18;
  while (--ptr2 >= ptr1)
    putchar(*ptr2);
  putchar('\n');
  }
% cc test.c
% a.out
!sklof ,lla s'tahT
%
```

What have we done here?  The assignment

```
ptr1 = "That's all, folks!";
```

sets `ptr1` to the address of the zeroth character of the string—in other words, it points to `'T'`.  Setting `ptr2` to `ptr1 + 18` points `ptr2` to the last character in the string, the invisible null.  This having been done, we then go around the loop as in our previous program.

If we think about it, this second version is a little mysterious. Where *is* the array that holds the characters in `"That's all, folks!"`?  We didn't declare one this time.  The fact is that `"That's all, folks!"` is a constant value, and that the assignment statement

```
ptr1 = "That's all, folks!";
```

is analogous to assignment statements like

```
    i = 1;
```

or

```
    c = 'x';
```

The characters in the string "That's all, folks!" are stored permanently as part of the function they appear in, just as the integer constant 1 or the character constant 'x' would be.

We've found that many programmers new to C often have a hard time getting used to the idea that byebye is exactly equivalent to &byebye[0], and that

```
    ptr1 = "That's all, folks!";
```

sets ptr1 to point to the address of the 'T' in "That's all, folks!". As often happens, it's C's shortcuts that are most confusing to the novice. You can ignore them if you want, but in fact nobody does; when you read production programs you'll never see

```
    &byebye[0]
```

What you will see is plain

```
    byebye
```

Like irregular verbs and marriage, C's shortcuts seem strange at first but they soon become second nature.

Finally, here's an example that goes a step farther, printing a string both forwards and backwards. Notice in this program that we don't need to supply a value that specifies the length of the string:

```
% cat test.c

/*
** Print a string forward and backward.
*/
main()
    {
    char *ptr1, *ptr2;

    ptr1 = ptr2 = "That's all, folks!";
    /*
       Seek to the end of the string,
       printing as you go.
    */
    while (*ptr2 != '\0')
       putchar(*ptr2++);
    /*
       Now seek back to the beginning
       of the string, still printing.
    */
    while (--ptr2 >= ptr1)
       putchar(*ptr2);
    putchar('\n');
    }

% cc test.c
% a.out
That's all, folks!!sklof ,lla s'tahT
%
```

## Manipulating Array Elements

Now we're in a position to look at more complex examples of the use of pointers. These examples involve a function, isitpal, which examines a string to see whether it's a palindrome. You know what a palindrome is, of course. It's a phrase that is spelt the same way backwards or forwards. There's one in the program on the opposite page.

What happens in main should be obvious to you by now. Calls are made to the function isitpal; the arguments are strings, which means that according to the rules of C we're sending isitpal pointers to the strings' zeroth elements. If isitpal sends back TRUE for a given string, we print a message identifying that string as a palindrome.

```
% cat test.c

#define TRUE 1
#define FALSE 0

/*
** Submit two strings to the palindrome test.
*/
main()
   {
   if (isitpal("FOURSCORE AND SEVEN YEARS") == TRUE)
     printf("string 1 is a palindrome\n");
   if (isitpal("ABLE WAS I ERE I SAW ELBA") == TRUE)
     printf("string 2 is a palindrome\n");
   }

/*
** Test a string for palindromia.
*/
isitpal(strptr)
char *strptr;
   {
   char *strptr2 = strptr;

   while (*strptr2 != '\0')              /* seek to end */
      ++strptr2;
   --strptr2;                            /* back up one char */
   while (strptr < strptr2)
                               /* compare mirror chars */
      if (*strptr++ != *strptr2--)
         return (FALSE);
   return (TRUE);
   }

% cc test.c
% a.out
string 2 is a palindrome
%
```

---

The function isitpal itself is almost as straightforward as our "That's all, folks!" examples. There are two pointers. strptr is set to the zeroth element of the target string and strptr2 is pushed forward till it finds the null character, then backed up one char so that it points to the last visible character in the string. (Again, this way we don't have to know the number of characters in the string.) After that it's simply a matter of comparing the characters that the two pointers point to as we move them closer together. When and if the pointers meet we stop, and declare the thing palindromic. Easy as pie.

But what if our palindrome isn't as neat as Napoleon's famous last words? In "ABLE WAS I ERE I SAW ELBA" the spaces are part of the palindrome, and we've capitalized everything so we don't have to worry about comparing lower- and upper-case letters. Which is being evasive. Mighty few palindromes are palindromic unless we agree to ignore spaces and capitalization and punctuation marks. For instance, there are the famous first words, "Madam, I'm Adam." So we need a couple of other functions, one to strip out non-alphabetic characters and blanks, and another to make all letters the same case. But at the same time we don't want our functions to change the strings. In general, unless there's an extremely good reason to do so, it's wise to avoid having a function change its argument. So our functions, which will filter out non-letters and turn lower case into upper case, will be written to avoid changing the arguments in `main`. Here's the program:

```
% cat test.c

#define TRUE 1
#define FALSE 0
#define MAX 80

char string1[] = "FOURSCORE AND SEVEN YEARS AGO";
char string2[] = "ABLE WAS I ERE I SAW ELBA";
char string3[] = "Madam, I'm Adam.";

/*
** Submit some strings to palindrome test.
*/
main()
    {
    printf("Palindromes:\n");
    if (isitpal(string1) == TRUE)
      printf("%s\n", string1);
    if (isitpal(string2) == TRUE)
      printf("%s\n", string2);
    if (isitpal(string3) == TRUE)
      printf("%s\n", string3);
    if (isitpal("Bei Leid lieh stets Heil die Lieb."))
      printf("Bei Leid lieh stets Heil die Lieb.\n");
    }
```

```
/*
** Test a string for palindromia.
*/
isitpal(strptr)
char *strptr;
   {
   char *lettersonly(), *ptr1, *ptr2;
   /*
      Set ptr1 and ptr2 to point to a copy of
      the string stripped of punctuation.
   */
   ptr1 = ptr2 = lettersonly(strptr);
   /*
      Seek to end of string, then back up one char.
   */
   while (*ptr2 != '\0')
      ++ptr2;
   --ptr2;
   /*
      Move both pointers toward the middle of the
      string, comparing letters as you go.  For
      purposes of comparison, use the upper-case
      equivalents of the letters.
   */
   while (ptr1 < ptr2)
      if (ltou(*ptr1++) != ltou(*ptr2--))
         return (FALSE);
   return (TRUE);
   }
```

```
/*
** Given a pointer to a string, return a pointer
** to a copy stripped of punctuation.
*/
char *lettersonly(strptr)
char *strptr;
   {
   char *ptr1, *ptr2;
   static char ourstring[MAX];
   ptr1 = strptr;
   ptr2 = ourstring;
   /*
     From beginning to end of the original string,
     copy only its letters into our new version.
   */
   while (*ptr1 != '\0')
      {
      if ((*ptr1 >= 'a' && *ptr1 <= 'z') ||
         (*ptr1 >= 'A' && *ptr1 <= 'Z'))
         *ptr2++ = *ptr1;
      ++ptr1;
      }
   *ptr2 = *ptr1;        /* copy the null terminator */
   return(ourstring); /* return ptr to new string */
   }


/*
** Given an ASCII character, return its
** upper-case equivalent.
*/
ltou(c)
char c;
   {
   if (c <= 'z' && c >= 'a')
      return (c + 'A' - 'a');
   else
      return(c);
   }


% cc test.c
% a.out
Palindromes:
ABLE WAS I ERE I SAW ELBA
Madam, I'm Adam.
Bei Leid lieh stets Heil die Lieb.
%
```

Obviously, if our filter functions `ltou` and `lettersonly` had changed the strings our program wouldn't have printed them out in their original form.

How does the program work? We know the function `ltou` already. Here we have it in the form that returns the upper-case equivalent of a single character rather than in the form that changes its argument.

But what about the function header `char *lettersonly(strptr)`? What are we to understand about the asterisk? Simple: the asterisk means that this function is going to return a *pointer* to a character string. In fact, `lettersonly` defines an array of its own, `ourstring`, which must not exceed **MAX** characters, into which it copies the nonblank, letters-only members of the array to which its argument points. (Note that `ourstring` is static—otherwise it would vanish when `lettersonly` was done.) In this way we avoid changing the argument. And then in `isitpal` we set `ptr1` and `ptr2` initially so they point to the copy of the original string—the pointer returned by `lettersonly`—and not to the original string itself.

## Notes on a Few Fine Points

We can write expressions like `*ptr1++` without ambiguity because the `++` and `*` operators associate from right to left: it's equivalent to writing `*(ptr++)`. We increment (or decrement) the *pointer*, not the thing being pointed to.

Also, we've defined **TRUE** as 1 and **FALSE** as 0. In fact, these definitions are redundant since C defines falsehood as zero and truth as anything else. So instead of

```
if (isitpal(string3) == TRUE)
```

we could simply have written

```
if (isitpal(string3))
```

but we have chosen the former style to make the code more readable. Unless you're pressed for space and time in your program, we recommend you do the same; but when you read C programs you'll often see the latter form.

Instead of

```
while (*ptr2 != '\0')
```

we could have written

```
while (*ptr2)
```

because '\0' is indeed equal to binary zero, and the expression *ptr2 becomes binary zero at the point we're using as our stopping place in the program. Again, the longer form makes the intent clearer, and it always pays to be as clear as possible.

Finally, we have C's logical OR operator ¦¦ in this program, which we have already discussed:

```
if ((*ptr1 >= 'a' && *ptr1 <= 'z') ¦¦
    (*ptr1 >= 'A' && *ptr1 <= 'Z'))
```

In this statement if *either*

```
(*ptr1 >= 'a' && *ptr1 <= 'z')
```

*or*

```
(*ptr1 >= 'A' && *ptr1 <= 'Z')
```

is true, then the entire if statement is true. The if statement is false only if *both* statements are false. This is the meaning of the logical OR.

# Chapter 11
# Control Structures II

In Chapter 6 we discussed two C control structures, the `while` and the `if-else`. To review briefly, here in pseudo-coding is the essence of the `if-else`:

```
if (this condition is true)
    {
    do this;
    and this;
    and this;
    }
else            /* the condition is false */
    {
    do this;
    and this;
    and this;
    }
```

and of the `while`:

```
while (this condition is true)
    {
    do this;
    and this;
    and this;
    }
```

The statements that follow the keywords if and while are executed
only if the conditional test is true. Thus, in a while such as

```
while (i >= j)
    {
    putchar(c);
    i = i - j;
    }
```

the statements within the curly braces will be executed over and over
for as long as the condition (i >= j) remains true.

On the other hand, the statements following an else are executed only if the conditional if-test is false.

There are three other control structures in C: the do-while,
the for, and the switch. These three control structures are in a
sense merely variations upon the if-else and the while, for anything we can do with them we can also do using the if-else or the
while. However, the do-while, for, and switch often allow
us to write our programs in a more convenient or logically clearer way.

### Looping in C Using the do-while

The do-while looks like this:

```
do
    {
    this;
    and this;
    and this;
    }
while (this condition is true);
```

A flowchart that shows how this control structure works is shown in
Figure 11.1. If you compare this illustration with the flowchart of the
while on page 77 you will see that the only difference between these
two control structures is the place where the conditional test is performed. The while tests its condition before executing any of its
statements; the do-while tests its condition after having executed its
statements. This means that the do-while will always execute its
statements at least once, even should its condition test false the first
time through. The while, on the other hand, assuming *its* condition
tests false immediately, will break out of its loop without once execut-

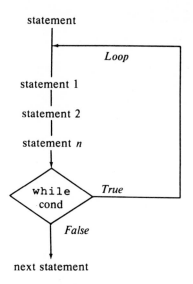

statement

statement 1

statement 2

statement *n*

while cond

*Loop*

*True*

*False*

next statement

**Figure 11.1.**

ing its statements. The following program points up this difference between the two control structures:

```
% cat test.c

main()
   {
   while (2 < 1)
      printf("I'm in the while loop.\n");
   do
      printf("I'm in the do loop.\n");
   while (2 < 1);
   }

% cc test.c
% a.out
I'm in the do loop.
%
```

The condition ( 2 < 1 ) is never true, of course, so the while immediately passes program control on to the do-while without executing its printf statement. But the do-while doesn't test its condition until after its printf statement has been executed, so

```
I'm in the do loop.
```

does get printed.

Apart from this peculiarity of the do-while, the while and do-while behave identically in a program.

Question: suppose we want to loop through both a do-while and a while five times? We know that if we write the condition of the while in this way:

```
main()
  {
  int i = 1;

  while (i <= 5)
     printf("%d\n", i++);
  }
```

the loop will be repeated five times. But what about the do-while? If we want its statements to be repeated five times must we write its condition as

```
while (i <= 5)
```

or as

```
while (i <= 4)
```

or what? Think about it. The answer is given at the end of this chapter.

do-while loops are fairly rare in C code since there are comparatively few occasions when we want to execute a loop at least once no matter what. Opposite is an example of where the do-while might be useful. One of C's library functions is strlen, which returns the number of characters in a string, not counting the terminating null. Suppose we want a variant of strlen (which we shall call strlen1) that, when we pass it a pointer to a string, returns the number of characters in that string, *including* the null. We know that every string has a length of at least 1 if we count the null terminator, so we're justified in assuming that we're going to go through the do-while at least once. In the case of the string "", we go through it exactly once.

```
% cat test.c

/*
** Exercise a new library function <strlen1>.
*/
main()
    {
    printf("%d\n", strlen1("now is the time"));
    printf("%d\n", strlen1("mama"));
    printf("%d\n", strlen1(""));
    }

/*
** Given a pointer to a string, return the length
** of the string, including the null terminator.
*/
int strlen1(sptr)
char *sptr;
    {
    int length;

    length = 0;
    do
        length++;
    while (*sptr++ != '\0');
    return(length);
    }

% cc test.c
% a.out
16
5
1
%
```

----

break and continue are used with the do-while just as they would be in a while construct. A break jumps you out of the loop, bypassing the conditional test. A continue sends you straight to the test at the end of the loop.

## Looping in C Using the for

Perhaps one reason so few C programmers use the do-while is that they are too busy using the for, which is probably the most popular looping control. The `for` allows us to specify three things about a loop on a single line: 1) the initial value of the counter; 2) the conditional test; 3) the value by which the loop is incremented or decremented. In pseudo-coding:

```
for (initialize counter; conditional test; reevaluate counter)
    {
    do this;
    and this;
    and this;
    }
```

The `for`, therefore, does exactly the same thing as this sequence of statements in the `while`:

```
initialize counter;
while (conditional test)
    {
    do this;
    and this;
    and this;
    reevaluate counter;
    }
```

So the following `while` loop

```
ptr = "string";
while (*ptr != '\0')
    {
    putchar(*ptr);
    ++ptr;
    }
```

is exactly equivalent to this `for` loop:

```
for (ptr = "string"; *ptr != '\0'; ++ptr)
    putchar(*ptr);
```

Both loops simply print "`string`" from beginning to end. The only difference between them is that in the `for` the initialization of the counter, the conditional test, and the incrementing of the counter are all specified on one line, within the parentheses, while in the `while` these parameters are on separate lines.

Now whether you use the `while` or the `for` is primarily a matter of taste. There will be times when the `while` seems more natural under the circumstances, there will be other times when the `for` seems more natural. It's up to you. Most C programmers use the `for` a lot, so, whether you use it yourself or not, you will undoubtedly find it used heavily in most of the C programs you read.

What you put within the parentheses is up to you. The two semicolons are invariant; they must *always* be present. However, the first and last parameters don't *have* to initialize and increment (or decrement) a counter, nor does the middle parameter *have* to be a conditional test. Any of these parameters can, in fact, be any valid C statement whatever—or it can be omitted altogether. The compiler does interpret the middle parameter as a conditional test, however, whatever it may actually do; that is, the middle parameter will always be evaluated as being true or false. (Recall that C defines false as a binary zero while true is defined as anything else.) The result of this characteristic of the `for` is that you can devise and run mad examples like the following:

```
% cat test.c

/*
** A mad example showing the sequence of
** events within a for-loop.
*/
main()
  {
  for (putchar('a'); putchar('b'); putchar('c'))
    putchar('d');
  }

% cc test.c
% a.out
abdcbdcbdcbdcbdcbdcbdcbdcbdcbdcbdcbdcbdcbdcbdcbdcbdc
%
```

This program may not be very useful but its output does show exactly how the flow of control runs through a `for` loop:

**a** represents the initialization (which is done only once) b represents the conditional test (which is repeated)

d represents statement execution (which is repeated every time the test is true)

c represents the incrementing (or, more generally, reevaluation) of the counter

all of which results in an unending series of bdc's. This particular loop would run forever because the function putchar not only prints its argument, it also returns it. So the value of putchar('b') in the conditional-test part of the loop will always return the value 'b', which is of course nonzero and therefore true by definition.

Perhaps the best way to demonstate the for's usefulness is to rewrite the programs we used to illustrate while loops. The program below is a revision of the example from page 81, with for's used in place of the while's. If you turn to page 81 and compare the two programs, we think you'll have to agree that the for version is easier to read and understand.

```
% cat test.c
/*
** Print all primes between 2 and 32767.
*/
main()
  {
  int i, n;

  for (n = 2; n <= 32767; ++n)
    {
    for (i = 2; i < n; ++i)
      if (n % i == 0)
         break;                      /* not a prime */
    if (i == n)
       printf("%d\n", n);      /* print the prime */
    }
  }
```

```
% cc test.c
% a.out
2
3
5
7
11
13
17
19
23
29
31
   .
   .
   .
%
```

As we said, all the semicolons within a `for` statement must be present though any or all three of the parameters may be omitted. As an extreme example, the statement

```
for (;;);
```

is an endless loop that does absolutely nothing—were a program to encounter such a statement, it would simply hang there forever. The reason is that the middle parameter, i.e., the conditional test, does not yield a binary zero, and so the loop would be repeated and repeated and repeated. For the same reason, the `for` control structure

```
for (;;)
   putchar('a');
```

would print an endless line of `a`'s, and so would

```
for (c = 'a';;)
   putchar(c);
```

assuming we had declared `c` as a `char`. On the other hand, the following loop is not endless, even though there are only two parameters within the parentheses:

```
for (ptr = "string"; *ptr != '\0';)
    putchar(*ptr++);
```

We've not forgotten to increment the counter; we've just sneaked the increment into the `putchar` statement.

## The Comma Operator

Another useful feature of the `for` is the comma operator , which extends the scope of the `for` by making it possible to include several expressions in either the initialization or the reevaluation parameters. (Incidentally, the comma operator is one of C's standard operators, but it is seldom used except to separate expressions within a `for`.) We've rewritten the palindrome program that appears on page 145 to show you how the comma operator is used. In fact, we've rewritten the program twice. The first revision (on page 161) merely shows how the program looks when written using the `for` in place of the `while`. The second revision (on page 162) is the same program, but altered slightly to illustrate the use of the comma operator. In both programs, the parameters of the `for` statement have been placed on separate lines for clarity.

```
% cat test.c

#define TRUE 1
#define FALSE 0

/*
** Submit two strings to the palindrome test.
*/
main()
    {
    if (isitpal("FOURSCORE AND SEVEN YEARS") == TRUE)
      printf("string1 is a palindrome\n");
    if (isitpal("ABLE WAS I ERE I SAW ELBA") == TRUE)
      printf("string2 is a palindrome\n");
    }


/*
** Palindromia test using for-loop without comma
** operators. The library function <strlen> is
** used to find the number of characters in the
** may-be-palindromic string.
*/
isitpal(strptr)
char *strptr;
    {
    char *strptr2;

    for (strptr2 = strptr + strlen(strptr) - 1;
      strptr < strptr2;
      strptr2--)
      if (*strptr++ != *strptr2)
        return(FALSE);
    return(TRUE);
    }

% cc test.c
% a.out
string2 is a palindrome
%
```

And on the next page is revision two showing the use of the comma operator. Note that we have to introduce a redundant variable, strptr1:

```
% cat test.c

#define TRUE 1
#define FALSE 0

/*
** Submit two strings to the palindrome test.
*/
main()
   {
   if (isitpal("FOURSCORE AND SEVEN YEARS") == TRUE)
      printf("string1 is a palindrome\n");
   if (isitpal("ABLE WAS I ERE I SAW ELBA") == TRUE)
      printf("string2 is a palindrome\n");
   }


/*
** Palindromia test using for-loop with comma
** operators. The library function <strlen> is
** used to find the number of characters in the
** may-be-palindromic string.
**
** The variable <strptr1> isn't necessary; we're
** using it to illustrate use of the comma oper-
** ator in the for-loop's initialization clause.
*/
isitpal(strptr)
char *strptr;
   {
   char *strptr1, *strptr2;

   for (strptr1 = strptr, strptr2 = strptr +
    strlen(strptr) - 1;
      strptr1 < strptr2;
      strptr1++, strptr2--)
      if (*strptr1 != *strptr2)
         return(FALSE);
   return(TRUE);
   }


% cc test.c
% a.out
string2 is a palindrome
%
```

break and continue statements can be used in a for just as they are in a while. The break immediately takes you out of the for loop while the continue brings the program back, in order, to the reevaluation counter, the conditional test, and then to the executable statements again. The following flowchart, which uses the while equivalent of the for for purposes of illustration, shows just where the continue returns the program for another execution of the loop.

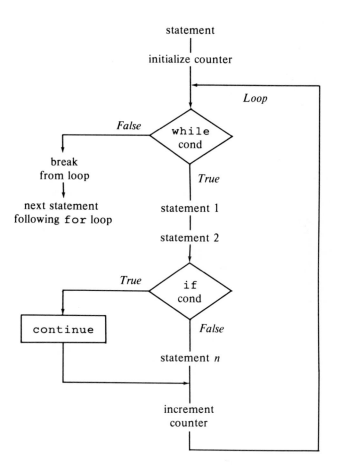

**Figure 11.2.**

As you see, the if-test determines whether or not a block of additional statements in the for will be bypassed. The continue thus provides another level of control within the structure. Compare this use of the `continue` with its use in the `while` as shown in the flowchart on page 84.

### Conditional Execution in C Using the `switch`

It often happens, in programming as in real life, that the choices we are asked to make are more complicated than merely selecting between two alternatives.  For example:

```
dial 123-4567
if nobody answers,
    hang up
else
    talk
```

is a simple alternative that corresponds to the `if-else`.  Or we can have a multiple-alternative situation such as this:

```
dial 123-4567
if a child answers,
    say "May I speak to your Mommy?"
else if a man answers,
    say "May I speak to your wife, mother or adult daughter?"
else if a woman answers,
    say "Good morning, Ma'am, I represent Nu-Goo Shampoo..."
else
    hang up
```

which, as you see, corresponds to a list of `if-else`'s.  We can of course make the list of alternatives arbitrarily long.  But since such lists occur frequently in programming, C provides a special control structure that allows us to handle them more expeditiously, using less code, and in a more regular format.  This control structure is the `switch`, more pedantically known as the `switch-case-default`, since these three keywords generally go together to make up the control structure. They most often appear as follows:

```
switch (integer expression)
   {
   case constant1 :
      do this ;
   case constant2 :
      do this ;

         .

         .

         .

   case constantn:
      do this;
   default:
      do this;
   }
```

The integer expression following the keyword `switch` is any C expression that will yield an integer value. It could be an integer constant like 1, 2, or 3; it could also be a function call or anything else that evaluates to an integer. It could also be, or yield, a character value, since as we know `char`'s are promoted automatically to integers. However the integer is obtained, you need its value as the criterion for selecting from among the alternatives available.

The keyword `case` is followed by an integer or a character constant. It could also be something more complicated, a constant expression like 3 * 2 or 'a' − 'A' that can be evaluated at compile-time—but that's getting too complicated; since this is a primer we'll stick to simple integers and characters. These values must all be different for the different `case` statements.

The "do this" lines in the pseudo-coding represent any legal C statement or statements.

What happens when you run a program containing a `switch`? First, the integer expression following the keyword `switch` is evaluated. The value it yields is then matched, one by one, against the constant values, or *labels,* that follow the `case` statements. When a match is found, the program executes the statement following that `case`, *and all subsequent* `case` *and* `default` *statements as well.* If no match is found with any of the case labels, only the statement following the `default` keyword is executed. A few examples will show how this control structure works. Consider the following program:

```
% cat test.c

main()
   {
   int i = 2;

   switch(i)
      {
      case 1:
         printf("I'm in case 1.\n");
      case 2:
         printf("I'm in case 2.\n");
      case 3:
         printf("I'm in case 3.\n");
      default:
         printf("I'm in default.\n");
      }
   }

% cc test.c
% a.out
I'm in case 2.
I'm in case 3.
I'm in default.
%
```

The control structure "switches" on the integer expression i, which of course evaluates to the integer value 2. This value matches the label for case 2, so the program prints . . . hey, what's this? It prints cases 2 *and* 3 *and* the default case? Well, yes. We said the switch executes the case where a match is found and all the subsequent cases and the default as well. There is an ancient rule in programming that says if you want a program to run faster or stay as small as possible, get the programmer to make some of the decisions that would otherwise have to be made by the computer. This is what happens with the switch: a certain amount of overhead is placed on the programmer in order to make things easier for the compiler. When the compiler finds a case that matches the integer expression you are using as a trigger, it will execute all the statements that follow that case clear to the end of the control structure. If you think that one case is enough, it's up to you to get out of the control structure then and there by using a break statement. The following example shows how it's done. Note there's no need for a break statement after the default, since it comes at the end anyway.

```
% cat test.c

main()
   {
   int i = 2;

   switch(i)
      {
      case 1:
         printf("I'm in case 1.\n");
         break;
      case 2:
         printf("I'm in case 2.\n");
         break;
      case 3:
         printf("I'm in case 3.\n");
         break;
      default:
         printf("I'm in default.\n");
      }
   }

% cc test.c
% a.out
I'm in case 2.
%
```

This falling-through-to-the-next-case is considered ugly by many users, but there it is. As a matter of fact, it can be useful if you want to deal with several cases in the same way, as we shall see later in this chapter.

Here's an example of the default statement in its usual catch-all role:

```
% cat test.c

main()
   {
   int i = 99;

   switch(i)
      {
      case 1:
         printf("I'm in case 1.\n");
         break;
      case 2:
         printf("I'm in case 2.\n");
         break;
      case 3:
         printf("I'm in case 3.\n");
         break;
      default:
         printf("I'm in default.\n");
      }
   }

% cc test.c
% a.out
I'm in default.
%
```

As you see, when no case applies, the program falls through to the default and executes *its* statement.

These examples may give you the wrong impression by implying that you can only use cases arranged in numerical order—1, 2, 3, default. You can in fact put the cases in any order you please; you can also use char values as case and switch labels. Here's an example of scrambled case order:

```
% cat test.c

main()
   {
   int i = 99;

   switch(i)
      {
      case 99:
        printf("I'm in case 99.\n");
        break;
      case 2:
        printf("I'm in case 2.\n");
        break;
      case 41:
        printf("I'm in case 41.\n");
        break;
      default:
        printf("I'm in default.\n");
      }
   }

% cc test.c
% a.out
I'm in case 99.
%
```

And here's an example that uses character constants as labels:

```
% cat test.c
main( )
    {
    char c = 'x';

    switch(c)
        {
        case 'a':
            printf("I'm in case 'a'.\n");
            break;
        case 'x':
            printf("I'm in case 'x'.\n");
            break;
        case 'z':
            printf("I'm in case 'z'.\n");
            break;
        default:
            printf("I'm in default.\n");
        }
    }
% cc test.c
% a.out
I'm in case 'x'.
%
```

You can mix integers and character constants if you wish.

If you switch on an integer value that doesn't match the labels of any of the cases, and if you have no default case, then the program simply falls through the entire switch and continues on with the next instruction that follows the control structure, if any:

```
% cat test.c

main( )
   {
   char c = 'b';

   switch(c)
      {
      case 'a':
         printf("I'm in case 'a'.\n");
         break;
      case 'x':
         printf("I'm in case 'x'.\n");
         break;
      case 'z':
         printf("I'm in case 'z'.\n");
      }
   }

% cc test.c
% a.out
%
```

We said there were times when the fall-through feature might prove handy. Here, for example, is a program that shows how different integer expression values will cause the identical statement to be executed:

```
% cat test.c

main( )
   {
   int i;

   for (i = 0; i <= 9; ++i)
      switch(i)
         {
         case 1:
         case 2:
         case 3:
         case 4:
         case 9:
            printf("%d is either 1, 2, 3, 4 or 9\n", i);
            break;
         case 5:
            printf("%d is of course 5\n", i);
            break;
         case 7:
         case 8:
            printf("%d is 7 or 8\n", i);
            break;
         default:
            printf("%d isn't 1, 2, 3, 4, 5, 7, 8, or 9\n", i);
         }
      }

% cc test.c
% a.out
0 isn't 1, 2, 3, 4, 5, 7, 8, or 9
1 is either 1, 2, 3, 4 or 9
2 is either 1, 2, 3, 4 or 9
3 is either 1, 2, 3, 4 or 9
4 is either 1, 2, 3, 4 or 9
5 is of course 5
6 isn't 1, 2, 3, 4, 5, 7, 8, or 9
7 is 7 or 8
8 is 7 or 8
9 is either 1, 2, 3, 4 or 9
%
```

As you see, in this program the `switch` is embedded within a `for` loop. With each repetition of the loop we switch on a different integer value. The program falls through the cases until a match between the switch value and a case label is found, whereupon the appropriate statement is printed. In a practical program, this technique can prove useful when a variety of conditions call for the same response.

## A Note on the `while` and `do-while`

There is no difference in the way a condition is specified in a `do-while` and a `while`. Suppose, for example, you want a loop repeated five times. The condition is written in exactly the same way for both control structures. First the `while`:

```
% cat test.c

main( )
  {
  int i = 1;

  while (i <= 5)
     printf("%d\n", i++);
  }

% cc test.c
% a.out
1
2
3
4
5
%
```

Then the `do-while`:

```
% cat test.c

main( )
  {
  int i = 1;

  do
     printf("%d\n", i++);
  while (i <= 5);
  }
```

```
% cc test.c
% a.out
1
2
3
4
5
%
```

# Chapter 12
# Structures

When we handle real-world data, we don't usually deal with little atoms of information by themselves—things like integers, character constants, and such. Instead, we deal with entities that are collections of things, each thing having its own attributes, just as the entity we call a "book" is a collection of things such as a title, an author, a publisher, chapters, pages, and words, each of which has its own attributes. For dealing with such collections, C provides a compound data type called a *structure*. A structure gathers together, in a fixed pattern, the different atoms of information that comprise a given entity. These atoms of information can be of any valid C data type, including other structures.

Before us as we write there is a pencil box containing three pencils. Let's organize these pencils into a C structure according to their attributes. Pencils have a hardness, of course, the hardness being classified according to a system of numbers—3 being relatively hard, 2 being softer, 1 being softer still, and so on. Pencils also have a manufacturer, like Eberhard Faber. And pencils have a number that identifies which model of the many different models in a company's product line we are talking about. These three pieces of information are stamped on nearly every pencil we buy. Examining our three pencils, we see we can characterize them as follows:

| Hardness | Maker | Number |
|:---:|:---:|:---:|
| 2 | Eberhard Faber | 482 |
| 0 | Gilbert | 33 |
| 3 | Eagle | 107 |

For convenience, let's abbreviate the manufacturers' names to single characters. We can now list the attributes of our pencils as follows:

        2, F, 482
        0, G, 33
        3, E, 107

## Structure Declarations

Now to translate this information into the form of a C structure. We will begin by declaring a structure we'll call `pencil`:

```
struct pencil
    {
    int hardness;
    char maker;
    int number;
    };
```

What you see here is called a *structure declaration*. The keyword `struct` tells the compiler that we are declaring a structure, of course. The name, or *tag*, of the structure declaration is `pencil`. The *members* of this structure are `hardness`, `maker`, and `number`. We know they are the members of this structure, and the only members, because they are enclosed by the pair of curly braces. Note that the closing brace is followed by a semicolon, which must *always* be present; we'll explain why on page 179. Finally, each member is declared to be of a specific data type.

It's important to understand from the beginning that, unlike the variable declarations we have discussed, a structure declaration does *not* tell the compiler to reserve any space in memory in which to store its members. All a structure declaration does is define the *form* of the structure; it acts as a *template* that describes the characteristics of the variables defined by this particular structure. Normally, structure declarations will appear at the head of the source code file, before any variables or functions are defined. In very large programs they're usually put into a separate header file, along with the `#define`'s.

## Variables of Type `struct`

Now that we've defined the structure template `pencil`, how do we use it to describe our three pencils? Well, there are quite a few ways in which we can do this. Let's begin with a fairly common way. Having written the structure declaration, we will use its tag to declare the variables defined by this structure:

```
% cat test.c

struct pencil               /* structure declaration */
    {
    int hardness;
    char maker;
    int number;
    };

main()
    {
    struct pencil p0, p1, p2;    /* var declarations */

    p0.hardness = 2;
    p0.maker = 'F';
    p0.number = 482;
    p1.hardness = 0;
    p1.maker = 'G';
    p1.number = 33;
    p2.hardness = 3;
    p2.maker = 'E';
    p2.number = 107;
    printf("The hardness of pencil 0 is %d.\n",
     p0.hardness);
    printf("The maker of pencil 1 is %c.\n", p1.maker);
    printf("The number of pencil 2 is %d.\n", p2.number);
    }

% cc test.c
% a.out
The hardness of pencil 0 is 2.
The maker of pencil 1 is G.
The number of pencil 2 is 107.
%
```

At this point we should say something about structure nomenclature. Unfortunately for C neophytes, both structure *templates* like pencil and structure *variables* like p0, p1 and p2 are commonly referred to as "structures." This breeds confusion, so let's take a minute to make clear exactly what we mean by these terms. In the declaration

```
struct pencil
    {
    int hardness;
    char maker;
    int number;
    };
```

what we're doing, as we've said, is creating a template that can be used like a cookie cutter to stamp out variables having identical characteristics. Each of the variables that conforms to this template will contain, in this fixed order, an `int` called `hardness`, a `char` called `maker`, and another `int` called `number`. These variables will, like every other C variable, be allocated space in memory under their names. This space will be large enough to hold values that will conform to the types specified by the template.

The name we gave our template was `pencil`, which we speak of as its *tag*. When we declare the structure variables

```
    struct pencil p0, p1, p2;
```

the tag `pencil` stands for the particular template the variables are to conform to. The tag is a kind of shorthand for

```
    {
    int hardness;
    char maker;
    int number;
    }
```

and it may be so used throughout the program. Which is to say we can always refer to the entire structure declaration simply by referring to its tag. If it weren't for the tag, we would have to declare the structure variables in the following way:

```
    struct
        {
        int hardness;
        char maker;
        int number;
        } p0, p1, p2;
```

Furthermore, we would have to write out this same structure declaration in its entirety in every function in which these variables must be declared:

```
struct
    {
    int hardness;
    char maker;
    int number;
    } p0;
    .
    .
    .
struct
    {
    int hardness;
    char maker;
    int number;
    } p1;
    .
    .
    .
struct
    {
    int hardness;
    char maker;
    int number;
    } p2;
    .
    .
    .
```

As you see, the existence of a tag is a great convenience. And note, incidentally, that the list of variable names ends with a semicolon. The semicolon marks the end of the list. A null list must also end with a semicolon because the compiler uses the semicolon to check whether a structure declaration does or does not include any variable names and, if it does, how many there are.

The price we pay for this convenience is the possibility of confusion, since (in terms of our example) programmers will casually refer to "the structure pencil" and to "the structure p0" when what they actually mean by the former phrase is "the structure template whose tag is pencil," and by the latter phrase "the variable whose data type is struct, whose template is pencil, and whose name is p0."

To avoid this kind of confusion we will always speak of "structure templates" (or "structure declarations") and of "structure variables" (which we will sometimes refer to as "records"). We promise never to talk about "structures" in general.

## The Assignment of Values to Structure Variables

According to the structure declaration in our program, the variables defined by that declaration share certain characteristics. Each variable is an entity, i.e., a *record*, with three members: an `int` called `hardness` that is followed by a `char` called `maker` that is followed by an `int` called `number`, in this exact order.

Every structure variable declared in our program may be assigned three values having these data types. These values are referenced by the following notation:

*structure_variable_name . member_name*

For example, in our program we refer to the `hardness` member of variable `p0` by writing `p0.hardness`, to the `maker` member of variable `p1` by writing `p1.maker`, and to the `number` member of variable `p2` by writing `p2.number`.

## Structure Variables and Arrays

Our program is rather simple-minded. All it does is assign values to the variables representing our three pencils, then print a few of those values for us to see. But that's all we intended to do anyway—show how structure variables are created and how we can then reference their individual members.

Here is a somewhat more sensible example of how structures are written. The following program more nearly resembles the sort of thing you'll encounter in actual programs, where structure templates are generally used to stamp out a number of records having identical characteristics. It should be apparent that our three variables `p0`, `p1` and `p2` can be thought of as three elements of an array and, in fact, structure variables almost always occur as arrays or lists. Wouldn't it simplify things if we declared an array of type `struct pencil` directly? It would. Let's modify our program so that variables `p0`, `p1` and `p2` are declared as the elements of an array we will call `p`:

```
% cat test.c

struct pencil
   {
   int hardness;
   char maker;
   int number;
   };

main()
   {
   int i;
   struct pencil p[3];

   p[0].hardness = 2;
   p[0].maker = 'F';
   p[0].number = 482;
   p[1].hardness = 0;
   p[1].maker = 'G';
   p[1].number = 33;
   p[2].hardness = 3;
   p[2].maker = 'E';
   p[2].number = 107;
   printf("  Hardness  Maker  Number\n\n");
   for (i = 0; i <= 2; ++i)
      printf("    %d     %c    %d\n",
         p[i].hardness, p[i].maker, p[i].number);
   }

% cc test.c
% a.out
    Hardness   Maker   Number

        2        F      482
        0        G      33
        3        E      107
%
```

The syntax we use to reference the members of each element of
array p is very much like the syntax we used in Chapter 9 to handle
arrays of int's and char's. For example, we refer to the zeroth
pencil's hardness as p[0].hardness, and we refer to the second
pencil's maker as p[2].maker. Does this seem an odd way to
describe the members of an array when they are part of a structure?

Think of it like this. Suppose we have three slips of paper. Each slip represents one record of the array **p**. On each slip are three lines of information corresponding to the three members of the structure template. If these three slips of paper are held together, and in order, by a spindle

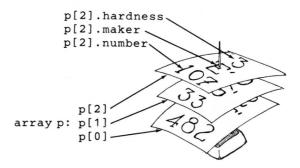

Figure 12.1.

what we have is a representation of the array **p**: a snapshot that shows what the contents of these three records are at a given instant of time, and the relation of these records to each other.

Let's summarize what we've discussed so far. We've described how structures are declared and we've shown how you can reference the individual members of structure variables, so you can either assign values to these members or look at their values. In many C compilers (but not UNIX C) those are about the only things you're allowed to do. You can't handle a structure variable as a whole. In other words, you can't assign structure variable **a** to structure variable **b** (unless you do it member by member), nor can you pass an entire structure variable as a function argument (though you can pass its individual members).

### Structure Variables and Pointers

But there *is* one other thing you can do that gives you a way around these non-UNIX limitations—you can take a structure variable's address. So you can pass a pointer to a structure variable as a function argument, thus indirectly passing the entire variable to the function.

What exactly is "a pointer to a structure variable"? Recall what we said in Chapter 9 about the name of an array standing for the address of its zeroth element. The same thing is true of the names of arrays of structure variables. The name of array **p** stands for the address of **p**'s zeroth element. As an example, look at the following variant of our program:

```
% cat test.c

struct pencil
    {
    int hardness;
    char maker;
    int number;
    };

main()
    {
    struct pencil p[3], *pen_ptr;

    p[0].hardness = 2;
    p[0].maker = 'F';
    p[0].number = 482;
    p[1].hardness = 0;
    p[1].maker = 'G';
    p[1].number = 33;
    p[2].hardness = 3;
    p[2].maker = 'E';
    p[2].number = 107;
    printf("   Hardness   Maker   Number\n\n");
    for(pen_ptr = p; pen_ptr <= p +2; ++pen_ptr)
        printf("      %d       %c     %d\n",
           pen_ptr->hardness, pen_ptr->maker,
           pen_ptr->number);
    }

% cc test.c
% a.out
    Hardness   Maker   Number

        2        F      482
        0        G      33
        3        E      107
%
```

We've modified our previous program by declaring a pointer **pen_ptr** which we can use (instead of the **p[i].hardness** notation) to run through the array when we want to print the hardness, maker, and model number of each record.

We wrote declarations for the array p and pointer `pen_ptr` on the same line, but of course we could have written them separately:

```
struct pencil p[3];
struct pencil *pen_ptr;
```

to better show what it is we are declaring. Just as the `char` declaration

```
char *c_ptr;
```

tells the compiler that the variable `c_ptr` is a pointer to data objects of type `char`, and just as the `int` declaration

```
int *i_ptr;
```

tells the compiler that the variable `i_ptr` is a pointer to data objects of type `int`, so the declaration

```
struct pencil *pen_ptr;
```

tells the compiler that the variable `pen_ptr` is a pointer to data objects of type `struct pencil`; that is, these data objects will have properties defined by the structure declaration `struct pencil`.

So, in the `for`-loop of our program, we begin by initializing the pointer `pen_ptr` to p. In other words, `pen_ptr` is set to point to the zeroth element of the array p. The pointer having been initialized, the first time we go through the `for`-loop, `printf` will print the values of the three members of structure variable `p[0]`, which we reference as

```
pen_ptr->hardness
pen_ptr->maker
pen_ptr->number
```

And what in the world do the `->` operators mean? It's quite simple, really. This is the way we *point to* a particular member of a structure variable. The general form is

   *name_of_pointer_to_structure_variable->member_name*

The $->$ is invariant. Though it is made up of a minus sign – and a greater-than sign $>$, it is considered a single symbol.

Let's take another snapshot of our data, this time including the pointer that is initialized to point to the head of the array p:

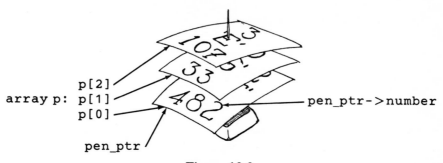

**Figure 12.2.**

Mind, this is a snapshot taken at the moment the for-loop is entered and **pen_ptr** initialized to p. So **pen_ptr->number** references the **number** member of the record being pointed to by **pen_ptr** at this moment, which is p[0]; which is to say that **pen_ptr->number** is just another way of writing p[0].number. At the next pass through the for-loop, **pen_ptr** will be incremented to point to the next record in the array, to p[1], so the expression **pen_ptr->number** will then be equivalent to p[1].number. In other words, our snapshot will then show

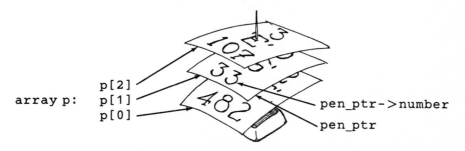

**Figure 12.3.**

And at the next pass through the for-loop, **pen_ptr** will point to p[2], so our snapshow will then show

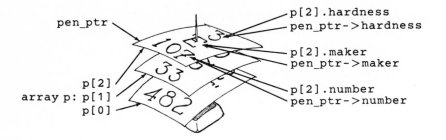

Figure 12.4

If that's still not clear, go back to our first program in this chapter (page 177). In that program we declared the structure variable p0, which has three members,

```
p0.hardness
p0.maker
p0.number
```

Now suppose in that program we had declared a pointer p0_ptr and set it to point to the address of p0:

```
struct pencil *p0_ptr = &p0;
```

In that case

p0.hardness *means the same as* p0_ptr->hardness
p0.maker *means the same as* p0_ptr->maker
p0.number *means the same as* p0_ptr->number

So the two notations are equivalent, and, to nail everything down, here's a program that proves it:

```
% cat test.c

struct pencil
    {
    int hardness;
    char maker;
    int number;
    };
```

```
main()
    {
    struct pencil p0;
    struct pencil *p0_ptr = &p0;

    p0.hardness = 2;
    p0.maker = 'F';
    p0.number = 482;
    printf("Hardness is %d %d\n", p0.hardness,
     p0_ptr->hardness);
    printf("Maker is %c %c\n", p0.maker, p0_ptr->maker);
    printf("Number is %d %d\n", p0.number, p0_ptr->number)
    }
```

```
% cc test.c
% a.out
Hardness is 2 2
Maker is F F
Number is 482 482
```

We declared the variable p0 to be of type struct pencil. We also declared a pointer *p0_ptr that points to the address of variable p0. When in the printf statement we print out the values referred to by the two different notations:

```
printf("Hardness is %d %d\n", p0.hardness,
 p0_ptr->hardness);
```

exactly the same value is printed out both times:

```
Hardness is 2 2
```

C production code relies heavily on structure pointers of this sort; what a programmer usually does is start by declaring a pointer like

```
struct pencil *p0_ptr = &p0;
```

and then refer to the member p0.hardness by writing

```
p0_ptr->hardness
```

as we did in the above program.

# Chapter 13
# Input/Output and Library Functions

Arranging for the input and output of data to and from a program is probably the ugliest part of programming. Many an elegant algorithm has lost its easy charm and turned sour when all the messy details of fetching data from the user's keyboard and returning results to his terminal are added to it. Furthermore, though a language designer may be able to conceive of a language that will do everything he wants it to do, it's quite a different thing to know what I/O (i.e., Input/Output) facilities to provide for the language, and how to incorporate these facilities in a practical way. It usually happens that a language must be used for a time before its designer knows how best to implement the I/O.

In Chapter 1 we described how Dennis Ritchie set out to design a minimal language. In keeping with that intention he deliberately omitted everything regarding I/O from his definition of the language. C simply makes no provision whatever for fetching data from anywhere outside a program or for sending data to anywhere outside a program. Of course I/O has to be confronted at some point—there's not much use in a program that spends all its time telling itself a secret. Here the users of C have an enormous advantage over the first users of languages like Fortran and Algol since from its inception C has always run under the control of an operating system, UNIX primarily, but now other operating systems as well, and all these operating systems have facilities for inputting and outputting data to and from the files and devices they support. It's quite a simple matter for a systems programmer to write a few small programs (in assembly language usually) that will put the C compiler in touch with a particular operating system's I/O facilities. Once that has been done, any good programmer can write functions that will perform any kind of input or output.

The developers of C did just that. They wrote a series of standard I/O functions and put them in a "library file" that everyone has access to. Though these functions weren't part of C's formal definition, they have become a *de facto* feature of the C language, and have been imitated faithfully by every designer of a non-UNIX C compiler. Whatever version of C you're using, it's almost certain that you have access to such a library of I/O routines.

Your system may not run under UNIX but Ritchie's system did, and the original C library was designed around the elegant I/O concepts built into UNIX. This shows up chiefly in a reliance on the idea of *standard input* and *standard output.* Think of them as streams of data passing through the computer. Your program doesn't know whether the input stream is coming from a user's keyboard, a card reader, a tape, a disk file, or some kind of telepathic hookup. Nor does your program know whether the output stream is going to a video screen, a printer, a card punch, a tape, a disk, or an industrial robot. Furthermore, it doesn't have to know. It's the operating system's job to make the particular connections. UNIX does this beautifully. Other operating systems, particularly those designed for the first microcomputers, make very heavy weather of it or they can't do it at all. In UNIX the default case is to take the standard input from the user's keyboard and to send the standard output to his terminal's printer or screen. In simpler operating systems these are often the only options.

If you have a non-UNIX system, check your user's manual to see how the standard I/O library routines are linked with your programs. On our reference computer we have to include a special switch, -1S (the "l" is a lower-case "ell") in our compile command:

```
cc test.c -1S
```

You'll be seeing this command a lot throughout the rest of this chapter.

Also for users of non-UNIX systems, in reading what follows be warned that other C designers have not always followed Ritchie's lead slavishly in the way they implemented their library routines. It is often difficult to emulate all the features of UNIX without an excessive cost in space, and many of the less-used functions available in UNIX C have been left out of non-UNIX-C implementations. Sometimes a designer is persuaded that his way of implementing an I/O routine is an improvement, or perhaps his operating system won't let him implement a routine in the same way, so there may be slight differences in the way that two versions of the same function work. We'll show you an example of this later. So if you are not running C under UNIX but under some other operating system, your I/O commands may produce results that are different from those of our examples. You must refer to your installation's user's manual to learn exactly how to use the C library functions that are available to you.

In this chapter we will discuss only six of the most common I/O functions (there are actually about forty all told), four string manipulation functions, and one conversion function. Because this is a primer, we won't broach the subject of file I/O at all. As it is, this chapter will be long enough.

### Terminal I/O Routines

These are the I/O routines we'll be describing:

```
getchar and putchar
gets and puts
scanf and printf
```

The first pair are used for character I/O, the second pair for string I/O, and the third pair for formatted I/O (i.e., data fitting a specific format). We've already used `getchar`, `putchar`, `gets`, and `printf`, so they should not be completely unfamiliar to you. As for the other two, `puts` is the seldom used complement to `gets`, and `scanf` is the *very* seldom used complement to `printf`. We will describe `scanf` because you *may* want to use it and because it looks a lot like `printf`, so it isn't all that hard to approach; but `scanf` is mostly a concession to those who cut their teeth on pre-C languages, and C programmers almost always manage to do without it.

### getchar and putchar

The first two library functions we'll deal with are `getchar` and `putchar`, and the first thing you should know about them is that they're not functions at all. In point of fact, they're macros similar to those discussed in Chapter 8. These macros expand into calls to two other, more general functions called `getc` and `putc`. But rather than confuse the issue, we'll discuss `getchar` and `putchar` just as if they were functions.

We may consider `getchar` as a function those header looks like this:

```
int getchar()
```

In other words, it takes no argument at all, and it returns a value of type `int`. The returned value is simply the value of the next ASCII character it encounters in the stream of ASCII characters coming from the standard input. (In terms of our limited purview, this would be the next character typed at your keyboard). As you can see, this is a very elementary function. It makes no assumptions about what it's going to find out there, and it dumbly returns with the character in its mouth like a faithful old retriever.

But wait. If `getchar` returns an ASCII character, why did we give its type as `int` and not as `char`? Because all `char`'s are promoted to `int`'s as returned values, as we mentioned on page 99. We just happen to know that the value of the `int` being returned will never exceed the highest ASCII character value allowed in our system.

`putchar` is the other side of the coin. Think of it as a function with a header like

```
putchar(c)
char c;
```

where the argument `c` is a `char`. We don't care about `putchar`'s type, since `putchar` doesn't get a character but instead sends one to the standard output (which, for our purposes, is the user's terminal).

Here is a simple illustration of `putchar` in action:

```
% cat test.c

/*
** Print all upper-case letters at user's terminal.
*/
main()
   {
   char c;

   for (c = 'A'; c <= 'Z'; ++c)
      putchar(c);
   }

% cc test.c -1S
% a.out
ABCDEFGHIJKLMNOPQRSTUVWXYZ%
```

There's really not much we can say about `putchar` that the example itself hasn't already said. Note that the % at the end of the output line isn't really output from the program. It's the UNIX prompt for the next command, and it appears on the same line as the output because we didn't output a newline in the program.

`getchar` is almost but not quite as simple. What do you make of this program?

```
A> type test.c

/*
** Echo input to output.
*/
main( )
   {
   for ( ; ; )
      putchar(getchar( ));
   }

A> cc1 test.c
BD Software C Compiler v1.44 (part I)
   38K elbowroom
BD Software C Compiler v1.44 (part II)
   33K to spare
A> clink test
BD Software C Linker  v1.44
Linkage complete
   45K left over
A> test
TThhee   rrooaadd   ooff f   eexxcceessss

lleeaaddss   ttoo   tthhee   ppaallaaccee

ooff   wwiissddoomm..

^C
A>
```

The program is country simple. It is an endless loop, and all that happens is that the computer receives the character sent from the user's keyboard (that's `getchar( )`) and sends it right back to his terminal (that's `putchar(c)`). So everything is echoed, including blanks and carriage returns. To get out of the program it was necessary to interrupt it with a control-C, which shows up as ^C.

Now, you will have noticed that this last example looks different from all the others in this book. In point of fact, it was not compiled by our reference compiler running under UNIX but by the BDS C compiler running on a CP/M-based microcomputer. Look what happens when we run the same code through our UNIX compiler:

```
% cat test.c

/*
** Echo input to output.
*/
main( )
    {
    for ( ; ; )
      putchar(getchar( ));
    }

% cc test.c -1S
% a.out
If the fool would persist in his folly
If the fool would persist in his folly
he would become wise.
he would become wise.
^C
%
```

Same program, same library function, different-looking results. Why? Because the operating-system environment is different. CP/M shoots a character right back to the user's terminal as the user types it. UNIX uses what's called buffered input, i.e., characters are accumulated in a temporary store until the user transmits a newline, then the whole line is digested and transmitted at one go. There's no denying that both versions of this program echo the input to the output, but they do it in very different ways. Let this example be a warning to you, and a reminder. The library functions we are discussing are *not* part of the C language definition and may vary from one implementation to another. Don't count on getting precisely the same results when you compile the same program at different installations.

## gets and puts

Now that we've had a look at `putchar` and `getchar`, let's go on to `gets` and `puts`. `puts` sends a string to the standard output, `gets` receives a string from the standard input. These two routines are quite simple. `puts` is seldom used, since it's easy enough to print a string using `printf`'s `%s` conversion command, as we will describe shortly.

    `puts` is a real function that has the following header:

```
int puts(string)
char *string;
```

The argument is a pointer to a string, and a string, of course, is a one-dimensional array of characters whose terminating character is a null— '\0'. Note that puts returns a value of type int. Why worry about the type of the returned value if the function's job is to send something out? Yet puts *does* return a value. If for any reason the system detects an error as it tries to write out the string, it will return the value EOF (i.e., End Of File), which in our version of UNIX is a constant that's defined as -1. So puts checks whether the computer is in fact doing what it's supposed to do.

puts doesn't *quite* copy a string to the standard output. What it actually does is copy all the characters except for the null terminator, which it replaces with a newline. So if you use puts to print the characters how now brown cow\0 what it actually sends is how now brown cow\n. The terminating null has been changed to a newline.

Here is an example of puts at work:

```
% cat test.c
/*
** Use library function <puts>
** to print a few strings.
*/
main()
   {
   static char string1[] = "abc";
   static char string2[] = "def\nghi\n";
   static char string3[] = "jkl";

   puts(string1);
   puts(string2);
   puts(string3);
   }
% cc test.c -1S
% a.out
abc
def
ghi

jkl
%
```

Note that each string is printed as a separate line because its invisible terminating null is replaced by an equally invisible newline. Including explicit newlines, such as those we've inserted in the second string, is perfectly legitimate; puts outputs the extra newlines just as it would any other character. Since string2 ends with an explicit newline— or, more correctly, since the newline is the last explicit character before the invisible null—*two* newlines are output and a blank line separates the printout of string2 from the printout of string3.

Why in this program did we specify the storage class of the string declarations as static? If we hadn't done so, the compiler would have considered the strings as automatic's, and you can't initialize an automatic array (refer to page 121). Since we wanted to initialize the strings in these declarations, we had to make them static.

As for gets, its header is

```
char *gets(string)
char *string;
```

which means its argument is a pointer to a string. gets gets the contents of that string from the user's terminal and simply returns a pointer to that same string. More exactly, the function gets a newline-terminated string from the user's terminal and replaces the newline with a null, which is necessary if the input is to be stored as a legitimate string. This means there's no way you can sneak a newline into that string. Every time you hit the carriage return key, gets thinks its job is done and runs off happily with what it believes is a complete string.

So if you type how now brown cow\n, gets will return a pointer to how now brown cow\0. Incidentally, remember to declare the string that gets takes as an argument.

If gets encounters an error condition, it will return an empty string (one containing only a null character). It will also return an empty string if you type only a carriage return. So when a program calls for user input, having the user enter a carriage return by itself as a response is a handy way of having him tell the program when he is finished inputting whatever he's inputting. Here's an example:

196   THE C PRIMER

```
% cat test.c

/*
** Get string from the user and display
** the decimal values of the constituent
** chars.  To halt, enter a null string
** (i.e., a carriage return by itself).
*/
main()
   {
   char string[80], *strptr;

   printf("When prompted, type a line.\n");
   do
      {
      putchar(':');        /* this is the prompt char */
      strptr = gets(string);
      do
         {
         printf("%c = %d\n", *strptr, *strptr);
         } while (*strptr++ != '\0');
                                   /* halt on null char */
      } while (*string != '\0');   /* halt on null */
   }


% cc test.c -1S
% a.out
When prompted, type a line.
: hello there
h = 104
e = 101
l = 108
l = 108
o = 111
  = 32
t = 116
h = 104
e = 101
r = 114
e = 101
  = 0
: who will   the cat?
w = 119
h = 104
o = 111
```

```
    = 32
w = 119
i = 105
l = 108
l = 108
    = 32
    = 7
    = 32
t = 116
h = 104
e = 101
    = 32
c = 99
a = 97
t = 116
? = 63
    = 0
: [c/r]
    = 0
%
```

(Our notation *[c/r]* indicates a carriage return typed by the user.)

There should be no surprises here. Because the program has been written in terms of `do-while` loops, we "see" the terminating nulls.

But why does the input sentence "who will    the cat?" have that double space in it? Well, we typed a control-G just between them, which is a non-printing ASCII character that rings the bell on our terminal. When we typed it, the bell rang, but that doesn't show up in print. The control-G went into the string because anything you can type will go right into `gets`, except for the carriage return. Note the decimal 7 in the listing. That's the bell. If you enter this program into your machine, and if it has a bell, you will hear a "ding" (or maybe a "beep") when you type the control-G. When `printf` sends that character back during the listing, your terminal will go "ding" again.

### printf and scanf

We've talked a lot about `printf` throughout this primer, and used it regularly, without having introduced it formally. Well, better late than never. In fact, we'll discuss both `printf` and its counterpart, `scanf`, which formats input. We should begin by saying that neither function is used very much in the kind of systems programming that C is usually used for, since compilers and editors and linkers and operating systems have almost no use for formatted input and output. How-

ever, you will find formatted output used in programs like report generators and in utility programs.  But scanf is used even less than
printf is; we are describing it mainly lest those familiar with other
programming languages get the idea that C provides no facilities whatever for formatted input.

    printf is provided to allow you to send formatted output to the
standard output.  Its function header looks like this:

```
printf(format_string, arg1, arg2, ... argn)
char *format_string;
```

Although the header shows a series of arguments, actually printf
has no way of knowing ahead of time how many arguments it's going to
get or what data types these arguments will have.  What printf does
is use the information contained in format_string to determine
how many arguments to expect, and what their types should be.  In the
following example

```
printf("The value of x is %d.\n", x);
```

format_string matches "The value of x is %d.\n", and
arg1 matches the real argument x.  The format string contains characters that are simply printed as they stand—The value of x is,
for example—and *conversion specifications* that begin with a percent sign,
like %d.  Each conversion specification will match one of the arguments
that follow the format string.  In this example, %d will match the argument x.  The d in %d is called the *conversion character.*  It tells
printf to print x as a decimal value.  Here is a complete list of the
conversion characters available in our compiler's version of printf
(remember, there's no guarantee that your printf will follow our
version exactly):

> *for integer arguments:*
> > d prints the argument as a decimal value
> > o prints the argument as an octal value
> > x prints the argument as a hexadecimal value
>
> *for floating-point arguments (i.e.,* float *or* double*):*
> > f prints the argument in the format *ddd.ddd,*
> > where *d* is a decimal digit
> > e prints the argument in the format *d.ddd±dd*

*for character arguments:*

    c prints the argument as a character value

*for string arguments:*

    s prints the string pointed to by the argument

These are *conversion* specifications, mind you, so it's all right to use, say, a %c with an integer argument, or a %d with a character argument. printf will do its best to perform the required conversion—from integer to character, character to integer, etc.—and print the result. If the output is nonsense, it's your fault, not the computer's.

We can provide optional specifiers in the conversion specifications:

| | |
|---|---|
| % | mandatory first character of the specification |
| – | minus sign for left-justified printout |
| *dd* | digits specifying field width |
| . | period separating field width (above) from precision (below) |
| *dd* | digits specifying precision |
| l | an "ell" character for long integer arguments |

These optional specifiers have to be given in a fixed order, and some will only work with certain conversion characters. Let's see what these characters mean and how they are used.

The *field width* specifier tells printf how many characters to use when printing an argument. For example, the conversion specification %9d says, "Print the argument as a decimal integer in a field nine characters wide." If the value happens not to fill up the entire field specified, the value is right-justified, that is, blanks are used on the left to pad the value out. If you should include the minus sign in a specification, this means left justification is desired, and the value will be padded with blanks on the right. Here is an example that should make everything clear:

```
% cat test.c

main()
   {
   char c = 'a';
   static char str[] = "how now";
   int i = 1234;
   float x = -123.456789;

   printf("|%c|%s|%d|%f|%e|\n", c, str, i, x, x);
   printf("|%2c|%8s|%5d|%12f|%-13e|\n", c, str,
     i, x, x);
   printf("|%-2c|%-8s|%-5d|%-12f|%-13e|\n", c, str, i,
     x, x);
   printf("|%0c|%6s|%3d|%10f|%11e|\n", c, str, i,
     x, x);
   }

% cc test.c -lS
% a.out
|a|how now|1234|-123.456787|-1.23457e+02|
| a| how now| 1234| -123.456787|-1.23457e+02 |
|a |how now |1234 |-123.456787 |-1.23457e+02 |
|a|how now|1234|-123.456787|-1.23457e+02|
%
```

We are using vertical bars instead of spaces as separators so you can
better see how the field width specifiers work. This program presents
several interesting features. The first call to printf has no field
width specifications at all: notice the result. The amount of space used
is exactly the amount required to print the values. But the floating-
point value of -123.456789 is printed by %f as -123.456787.
Why the error? Well, the specifier for floating-point values, %f, is
guaranteed to show only six decimal places in a result, unless, as we'll
show in a moment, you specify otherwise. But a floating-point variable
just doesn't have enough bits stored in memory to give you a result accurate to six decimal places. As you see, the last decimal place is in-
correct. On the other hand, the %e conversion specification rounds
this floating-point value up to -1.23457e+02, which is equivalent
to -123.457. Why *this* error? Because %e is guaranteed to show only
five decimal places after the decimal point, which in this case means
the value has to be rounded. Which is nice in a way; %e produces
more accurate results.

We could of course cure this precision problem by declaring the variable x to be a double and not a float.  If we were to do so, we would have this output:

```
┆a┆how now┆1234┆-123.456789┆-1.23457e+02┆
```

(Incidentally, notice that C doesn't have a separate conversion specification for double's.)

Continuing, in the second call to printf we specified field widths that gave everything one extra space.  Notice that everything is automatically right justified.

In the third call to printf, we've also given everything one extra space, but because we used the minus sign in the specification, everything has been left-justified.

In the fourth call to printf, all the width specifications are too small for any of the values to be printed in full, yet printf goes right ahead and prints them anyway, its output being a duplicate of the output of the first printf.  printf has been designed so that you won't lose anything if you write the wrong field width specification.  When there's a conflict between field width and the amount of space required to print a value, printf will ignore the field width specifications instead of truncating a value or printing out an error message.  Which is quite sensible.

Using printf, we can also specify the *precision* with which results are printed.  The precision of a float or double in this sense is the number of decimal places specified in a %f conversion specifier, or the number of digits specified (both to the left and to the right of the decimal point) for a %e conversion specifier.  For a string, the precision is the number of characters to be printed.  Here's an example of precision specification:

```
% cat test.c

main()
   {
   char c = 'a';
   static char str[] = "how now";
   int i = 1234;
   float x = -123.456789;

   printf("|%13.2f|%13.2e|\n", x, x);
   printf("|%13.0f|%13.0e|\n",x, x );
   printf("|%13.26f|\n", x);
   printf("|%40.32f|\n", x);
   printf("|%6.1c|%6.1d|\n", c, i);
   printf("|%8.3s|%8.1s|%8.0s|\n", str, str, str);
   }

% cc test.c -1S
% a.out
|    -123.46|    -1.2e+02|
|      -123|      -.e+02|
|-123.4567871093750000000000000|
|  -123.45678710937500000000000000000000|
|    a| 1234|
|   how|      h| how now|
%
```

These results should speak for themselves, but we'll say a few words about them anyway. In the first printf, the %13.2f and %13.2e conversion specifications specify that the results appear in fields that are thirteen characters wide, with two decimal places in the case of -123.45, and two digits overall in the case of -1.2e+02. Well, you get what you ask for, with the blank spaces padded out on the left of the results.

In the second call to printf, asking for zero precision gives no decimal places (and no decimal point) in -123, and no digits at all in -.e+02. The latter result is useless but the former might be valid for some purpose. The third and fourth calls to printf allow ridiculously optimistic specifications: %40.32f really does print a result to thirty-two decimal places in a field forty characters wide; never mind that most of the characters are zeros. And note that %13.26f prints the result to twenty-six places even though it has to ignore the field width specification to do so. Precision takes precedence.

As for trying to specify precision for a char and an int, as shown in the fifth call to `printf`, the precision specification is simply ignored, though the field width is taken as given. Finally, in the last call to `printf`, you can see how precision works with a string. Note that the specification `%8.0s` doesn't suppress the string as you might expect; on the contrary, the 0 is ignored and the whole string is printed, just as if we'd specified `%8s`.

So far we've been describing `printf`'s specifications as if we had to use `%s` for a string, `%d` for an integer, `%c` for a character value, and so on. This isn't true at all. `printf` takes these specifications and attempts to perform the specified conversions, and it will do its best to produce whatever value you have specified. Sometimes the result is very useful, as on page 196 where we printed the same value as both a character and a decimal to show the numeric values of ASCII characters. Sometimes the result is nonsense, as when trying to print a string as an integer value. Sometimes the result is disastrous and your entire program blows up. The following program shows some of these conversions, some sensible, some weird. We don't try to show every possible combination because some would indeed blitz the program.

```
% cat test.c
main()
    {
    char c = 'a';
    static char str[] = "how now";
    int i = 1234;
    float x = -123.456789;

    printf("%c|%d|%f|\n", c, c, c);
    printf("%s|%d|%f|\n", str, str, str);
    printf("%c|%d|%f|\n", i, i, i);
    printf("%f|%d\n", x, x);
    }
% cc test.c -lS
% a.out
a|97|0.000000|
how now|1412|0.000000|
R|1234|0.000000|
-123.456787|-15370
%
```

We'll leave you to analyze the results by yourself; some of the conversions are quite sensible.

Let's now turn our attention to scanf. scanf is provided to allow you to read in data from standard input that is formatted according to your own specifications. As we said, there aren't many applications where you'll find this facility useful. It's really a hangover from the days when data came from punched cards and the Fortran or Cobol program you were using had painfully precise specifications that told you exactly how to read each field on each card—you know, the first twenty characters represented the customer's name, the next four characters were his street address, the next sixteen the street name, etc., etc., etc.

scanf's function header looks like this:

```
int scanf(format_string, argptr1, argptr2, . . . argptrn)
char *format_string;
```

Like printf, scanf has a variable number of arguments. However, there's an important difference: scanf's arguments are *pointers* to values in the calling program. Pointers are necessary because scanf is going to change certain variables by getting values from the user and dropping them into the variables specified, and (remember Chapter 7) you can change the value pointed to by an argument but not the argument itself.

The format string in scanf is interpreted somewhat differently than the format string of printf. scanf's format string tells scanf what kind of input to expect. When you give it a character (but not a blank, tab, newline, or %), scanf expects to match that character as it reads the input. When you give it whitespace (i.e., a blank or tab or newline), scanf takes that whitespace as a signal to read input for as long as the next character isn't whitespace. When you give scanf a % symbol followed by certain conversion specifications, scanf takes that specification as a signal to convert the field it's looking at in accordance with your specifications.

Here is a list of the conversion symbols available in our compiler's version of scanf (remember, your compiler's version may differ):

*for integer input:*

d   tells scanf to expect a decimal value

o   specifies an octal value

x   specifies a hexadecimal value

*for floating-point input:*

e,f   tell `scanf` to expect
       a floating-point value—
       e and f are synonymous and either will accept a
       value that looks either like 12.34 or 1.2e3

*for character input:*

c      specifies a single character, which may be a blank (despite
       what we said above about skipping blanks)

*for string input:*

s      specifies a string, that is, a series of characters terminated
       by a newline or a space

There are in addition two other specifiers you can use in a `scanf` conversion specification. One is a field-width specifier. The other is the *assignment suppression character* \*, which tells `scanf` to ignore a field specification.

Here is an example that should make things clearer:

**% cat test.c**

```
main()
    {
    char achar;
    char string[64];
    int aint;
    float afloat;

    scanf("%c %d %s %f", &achar, &aint, string, &afloat);
    printf("%c %d %s %f\n", achar, aint, string, afloat);
    }
```

**% cc test.c -lS**
**% a.out**
**x 123 hello 123.456**
x 123 hello 123.456001
%

The format string tells `scanf` to be on the lookout for a single character to put into `achar`, then to move on to the next non-blank, non-tab, non-newline character in the input stream (this is what the blank after %c specifies), and at that point to begin looking for a decimal integer to stuff into `aint`; then to move on to the next non-whitespace character and begin looking for a string. Note that the string is of undefined length. `scanf` simply assumes that the string ends with the first whitespace encountered after it begins. In this case that will be the blank that follows `hello`. Finally `scanf` moves to the next non-whitespace character and starts putting floating-point input into `afloat`. And why did we specify plain `string` instead of `&string`? Because `string` is already defined as a pointer to the head of the string (see page 141).

Since a newline qualifies as whitespace, the user's newline ends the floating-point input. That satisfies the format string specification, and `printf` then shows what values were put into our variables.

It's important to realize that `scanf` sees all input as a single stream of characters that includes the final newline. For example, consider this run of the above program:

```
% a.out
x 123
hello
123.456
x 123 hello 123.456001
```

The input that `scanf` sees is:

```
x 123\nhello\n123.456\n
```

As the output shows, both the newlines and blanks qualify as whitespace.

Or consider this run:

```
% a.out
x123hello123.456
1
x 123 hello123.456 1.000000
```

How did `scanf` know where to cut the input stream? Well, a single character is one character, so that takes care of the initial `x`; since the letter h isn't part of any integer, `scanf` halts the integer input after `123`. But a string can contain anything, so `scanf` stuffs character after character into `string`, going right through `123.456` and ending only when it hits whitespace, in this case a newline. The next character, the `1`, is then taken to be a floating-point value that goes into `afloat`. It's clear enough when you know what's happening.

The %c specifications can be tricky.  Can you figure out why we get the following results?

```
% a.out
[c/r]
123 hello 123.456

  123 hello 123.456001
%
```

Well, our input stream was

```
\n123 hello 123.456\n
```

so the character that went into achar was the first newline, which printf faithfully printed as a blank line.

Suppose we don't tell scanf to skip whitespace:

```
% cat test.c

main()
    {
    char achar;
    char string[64];
    int aint;
    float afloat;

    scanf("%c%d%s%f", &achar, &aint, string, &afloat);
    printf("%c %d %s %f\n", achar, aint, string, afloat);
    }

% cc test.c -lS
% a.out
x 123 hello 123.456
x 123 hello 123.456001
% a.out
x 123
hello
123.456
x 123 hello 123.456001
% a.out
x123hello123.456
1
x 123 hello123.456 1.000000
```

```
% a.out
[c/r]
123 hello 123.456

 123 hello 123.456001
%
```

Those examples show that any whitespace in your input stream serves only to separate the input items, unless you intentionally read it in with a %c specification.

The following shows how you can skip a field using the assignment suppression character:

```
% cat test.c
main()
   {
   int aint;
   float afloat;

   scanf("%d %*d %f", &aint, &afloat);
   printf("%d %f\n", aint, afloat);
   }

% cc test.c -lS
% a.out
123 456 78.901
123 78.901001
%
```

And this shows how field width specifications are used with scanf:

```
% cat test.c

main()
   {
   char achar;
   char string[64];
   int aint;
   float afloat;

   scanf("%c%3d%*2d%6s%2f", &achar, &aint, string,
    &afloat);
   printf("%c %d %s %f\n", achar, aint, string, afloat);
   }
```

```
% cc test.c -lS
% a.out
12345678901234
1 234 789012 34.000000
%
```

You can almost hear `scanf` talking to itself: "I need a single character, that's 1. Next I want three decimal digits, that's 234. Next I read in a six-character string, which is 789012. And the next two characters are going to be converted to floating point; they're 34, so I have 34.000000." Here is a more elaborate example:

```
% cat test.c

main()
   {
   char achar;
   char string[64];
   int aint;
   float afloat;

   scanf("%c%3d%*2d%6s%2f", &achar, &aint, string,
    &afloat);
   printf("%c %d %s %f\n", achar, aint, string, afloat);
   scanf("%c%2d%3f", &achar, &aint, &afloat);
   printf("%c %d %f\n", achar, aint, afloat);
   }

% cc test.c -lS
% a.out
12345678901234
1 234 789012 34.000000
12345678901234

  12 345.000000
%
```

What went wrong? The output doesn't at all look like what we specified in the input. Well, the first input stream is this:

```
12345678901234\n
```

After we type in the first line and end it with a carriage return, the first call to `scanf` chomps through the input and produces what we expect:

```
1 234 789012 34.000000
```

So we type in the second input line:

```
12345678901234\n
```

But if you look closely, you will see that the program hasn't yet dealt with the newline that ended our first input line. scanf doesn't throw it away. Nothing is ever thrown away unless we deliberately demand it by using the assignment suppression character *. So the next call to scanf begins by scanning that newline character. That is, the newline is assigned to achar on the second call to scanf, so the two-digit integer becomes 12, and the three-digit float becomes 345.000000. scanf isn't being tricky. It is in fact very literal-minded and predictable, but it can surprise you if you're not on your toes.

In our next example, we want scanf to match non-whitespace, non-conversion characters in the format string:

```
% cat test.c

main()
  {
  int int1, int2, int3;

  printf("%d\n", scanf("%d-%d-%d", &int1, &int2,
  &int3));
  printf("int1 = %d, int2 = %d, int3 = %d\n", int1,
  int2, int3);
  }

% cc test.c -1S
% a.out
123-45-6789
3
int1 = 123, int2 = 45, int3 = 6789
% a.out
123-45 6789
2
int1 = 123, int2 = 45, int3 = 0
% a.out
123,45-6789
1
int1 = 123, int2 = 0, int3 = 0
%
```

The characters to be matched in this program are the dashes. Note in the sample run that printf is used to show the integer value of the call to scanf itself. How do we interpret this value?

Well, we said that all I/O routines should perform some error checking, which scanf does by returning the count of data items it has successfully found. In the first run of the program it found all three. In the second run the second dash didn't get matched with any-thing, so scanf found only two data items. In the third run the first dash didn't get matched, so the program terminated without looking any further, returning the value 1.

You can combine field widths with character matching to enforce a strict format via scanf. In the next program, scanf will return a value of 3 only if you enter a number in social-security format (i.e., *ddd-dd-dddd*):

```
% cat test.c

main()
    {
    int int1, int2, int3;

    printf("%d\n", scanf("%3d-%2d-%4d", &int1, &int2,
      &int3));
    printf("int = %d, int2 = %d, int3 = %d\n", int1, int2,
      int3);
    }


% cc test.c -1S
% a.out
123-45-6789
3
int = 123, int2 = 45, int3 = 6789
% a.out
12-345-6789
2
int = 12, int2 = 34, int3 = 0
% a.out
123-456-789
2
int = 123, int2 = 45, int3 = 0
%
```

### String-Handling Functions

We shall discuss the following string-handling functions:

strcat   concatenate two strings
strcmp   compare two strings
strcpy   copy one string over another
strlen   find the length of a string

There are many other string-handling functions, but these are the most commonly used, and will illustrate string-handling in general.

### strcat

strcat's function header looks like this:

```
char *strcat(string1, string2)
char *string1, *string2;
```

As you see, both arguments are strings (that is, pointers to the zeroth element in a character array) and the returned value is a string pointer too; more specifically, the returned value is identical to the first argument. What strcat does is butt two strings together. It does so by removing the null terminator at the end of string1 and beginning a copy of string2 there. Here is an example that shows how strcat is used:

```
% cat test.c

main()
    {
    static char str1[21] = "How now,";
    static char str2[] = " brown cow.";

    printf("%s\n", strcat(str1, str2));
    }

% cc test.c -1S
% a.out
How now, brown cow.
%
```

If we assume that both strings are stored in memory as shown, str1 will be initialized to How now,\0 and str2 to  brown cow.\0.

The call to `strcat` puts the two strings together and returns a pointer to `str1`, which now contains `How now, brown cow.\0`. The string at `str2` remains unchanged.

You must be sure you leave enough space in `str1` to accomodate the final string, which is why in the program we specified the size of the final array in `str1`'s declaration. If we hadn't, the compiler would have allotted exactly enough space to hold `"How now,"` and no more.

Here is a variation on this program in which `str2` is not stored as a variable but as a string constant coded right into the program:

```
% cat test.c

main()
    {
    static char str1[21] = "How now,";

    printf("%s\n", strcat(str1, " brown cow,"));
    }

% cc test.c -1S
% a.out
How now, brown cow.
%
```

As you see, the output is identical to our first version.

## strcmp

`strcmp` compares two strings. Its header looks like this:

```
int strcmp(string1, string2)
char *string1, *string2;
```

The two strings identified by the arguments are compared letter by letter until either there is a mismatch or one of the strings terminates in a null character, whichever comes first. If the two strings are the same, `strcmp` returns a value of zero. Otherwise, it returns the numeric difference between the nonmatching character in `string1` and the character in `string2`, as we described in the last chapter. Here is a program that shows the differences that can occur:

```
% cat test.c

main()
    {
    printf("%d\n", strcmp("hello", "hello"));
    printf("%d\n", strcmp("jello", "hello"));
    printf("%d\n", strcmp("hello", "hello there"));
    }

% cc test.c -1S
% a.out
0
2
-32
%
```

In the first call to printf, the two strings are identical—"hello" and "hello"—and the result is zero. In the second call to printf, the first character of "jello" doesn't match the first character of "hello", and the result is 2, which is the numeric difference between ASCII 'j' and ASCII 'h': i.e., 'j' minus 'h' equals 2. In the third call to printf, "hello" doesn't match "hello there" because the null terminator at the end of the first "hello" doesn't match the blank in "hello there". The value returned is -32, which is the value of the null character (zero) minus the value of the ASCII space: i.e., '\0' minus ' ' equals −32.

The exact value of the mismatch will rarely concern us. All we usually want to know is whether or not the first string is alphabetically above the second string. If it is, a positive value is returned; if it isn't, a negative value is returned. Any nonzero value means a mismatch.

## strcpy

strcpy gives us a way around the lack of a string-assignment operator in C. Here is its function header:

```
char *strcpy(string1, string2)
char *string1, *string2;
```

The string pointed to by string2 is copied, character by character, into the area pointed to by string1. This isn't a matter of changing or moving pointers; the characters really do get copied. The source of the copied characters, string2, remains unchanged. The function returns its first argument, a pointer to the newly copied string.  Here is an example of what `strcpy` does:

```
% cat test.c

main()
   {
   char str1[21];

   strcpy(str1, "How now, brown cow.");
   printf("%s\n", str1);
   printf("%s\n", strcpy(str1, "a b c"));
   }

% cc test.c -lS
% a.out
How now, brown cow.
a b c
%
```

In the first call to `strcpy` we make the second argument a string constant.  As the first call to `printf` shows, `str1` has indeed been stuffed with the characters you'd expect.  The second call to `printf` makes use of the fact that `strcpy` returns its first argument unchanged.  It also shows that we can copy a newer, shorter value into the same array.  Note that we get "a b c" the second time around and not "a b cow, brown cow." because the null pointer at the end of the second argument is copied as part of the string.

## strlen

Finally, `strlen`'s header looks like this:

```
int strlen(string)
char *string;
```

`strlen` simply returns the number of characters in the string, *not counting the null terminator at the end.*  Here is an example of `strlen` in action:

```
% cat test.c

main()
    {
    static char str1[] = "Oho, roan doe.";

    printf("%d\n", strlen(str1));
    printf("%d\n", strlen("Oho, roan doe."));
    printf("%d\n", strlen("abc\0def"));
    printf("%d\n", strlen(""));
    }

% cc test.c -lS
% a.out
14
14
3
0
%
```

As you see, `strlen` works with both string variables and string constants. Note also that the length of `"abc\0def"` is only 3, since the string count ends at the first null. Finally, note that the length of the null string `""` is zero.

### Converting Characters to Integers

We want finally to mention a library function that is used to convert strings to integers. This is `atoi`, which converts ASCII characters to integer values. In other words, you can use it to transform a string value like `"12345"` to the integer value `12345`. Here is the function header of `atoi`:

```
int atoi(string)
char *string;
```

Given a string containing decimal numbers, `atoi` returns the integer equivalent. There may be any number of tabs and spaces preceding the number, and it may begin with a minus sign if the quantity is negative. The number ends either with the null terminator or with any other non-digit value. Here is a sample program:

```
% cat test.c
main()
   {
   printf("%d\n", atoi("123"));
   printf("%d\n", atoi("+123"));
   printf("%d\n", atoi("-123"));
   printf("%d\n", atoi("000000000123"));
   printf("%d\n", atoi("   123"));
   printf("%d\n", atoi("123   "));
   printf("%d\n", atoi("3.4"));
   printf("%d\n", atoi("123abcd"));
   printf("%d\n", atoi("123456789"));
   }
% cc test.c -1S
% a.out
123
0
-123
123
123
123
3
123
-13035
%
```

The conversions of "123", "+123" and "-123" occur as expected
(recall that the plus sign + is meaningful in C only as an addition
operator). The leading zeros of "000000000123" have no effect on
the digits output. Neither have the leading blanks of "   123". Since
neither a blank nor a '.' nor the letter 'a' is a digit, the strings
"123   ", "3.4", and "123abcd" come out as 123, 3, and 123,
respectively. The final printf produces weird results because we
can't stuff a value as large as "123456789" into an integer.

So endeth the C primer. Readers who have stayed with us to the end
know enough now to write very effective C programs. We suggest that
you begin programming in C as soon as possible—that's really the only
way to get the hang of it.

# Appendix
# A Budget of Omissions

The features of C that we have omitted from the primer proper are divided into sections that match the chapters of the book.

## Chapter 3: Primary Data Types

We left out `short` and `unsigned` integers. They're used in declarations this way:

```
short int x;
unsigned int y;
```

Depending on the machine and the compiler, short integers may or may not take less storage and offer a smaller range than "normal" integers or `long`'s. An `unsigned` integer takes just as much space as in `int`, but it has magnitude only—it can't be negative. This allows you to count twice as high, of course.

As for constants, we didn't mention long constants, and we didn't mention hexadecimal and octal notation for constants. If an integer constant begins with a zero, C reads it as an octal number; if it begins with a zero plus an x—0x or 0X—C reads it as a hexadecimal number. For example, 010 is the octal equivalent of the decimal constant 8. Hex values may contain the digits a through f, or A through F. For example, 0x1f is the hex equivalent of the decimal constant 31.

An explicitly long constant is represented by tacking 1 or L on to it as a prefix; C assumes that all constants larger than the largest "normal" int represent `long` values.

219

## Chapter 4: Storage Classes

There's a C convenience called `typedef` that masquerades as a storage class. `typedef` can be used wherever you can use keywords like `auto` or `static`. It is in a way reminiscent of `#define`, in that it allows you to create synonyms for C types which already exist. For example,

```
typedef int *INTEGER_POINTER;
```

creates a new "type," `INTEGER_POINTER`, which may be used in subsequent declarations, so that

```
INTEGER_POINTER x, y, z;
```

is exactly equivalent to

```
int *x, *y, *z;
```

This kind of metonymy is beyond the power of `#define`.

## Chapter 5: Operators

Here, very briefly, are the operators we've ignored.

The `cast` operator forces type conversion. It takes the form

(*type*) *expression*

and it returns the value of *expression* as the specified *type*. For example, `(char *)x` returns the value of `x` as if `x` were a character pointer, no matter what `x` was declared as originally. The value of `x` itself is unchanged.

`sizeof` is an operator that does its work when a program is compiled, not when it's run. It simply returns the size of its single operand in bytes. The operand may be a data object (typically the name of an array or structure) or it may be one of C's primary or derived data types. If we've defined `int ra[7]`, then `sizeof(ra)` yields 14 for our reference computer, while `sizeof(int *)` yields a value of 2.

The *conditional operator* `? :` is sometimes called the *ternary operator* because it takes three arguments. In fact, it's a kind of foreshortened `if-then-else`. Its general form is *expression1*? *expression2* : *expression3*

If *expression1* is non-zero, then the value returned is that of *expression2*; otherwise the value returned is that of *expression3*. The statement

```
printf("%c", (c >= ' ') ? c : '?');
```

will print c as a character if c's value is greater than or equal to an ASCII blank; otherwise it prints a question mark.

C provides facilities for dealing with data objects as explicit strings of bits. Of course, in the final analysis all computer operations deal with bit strings, but C's bitwise operators give the programmer direct control over the pattern of bits that form character or integer values.

~ is the *one's-complement* operator. It's *unary*—in other words, it works on only one operand—and its function is to return its operand's one's-complement value. This means that every 0 bit in the operand's binary representation is made a 1 while every 1 becomes a 0. The operand must be of type **char** or **int**.

The *left shift* operator $<<$ and the *right shift* operator $>>$ take the general forms

*expression1* $<<$ *expression2*
*expression1* $>>$ *expression2*

where *expression1* is taken as a bit string to be shifted left or right by the number of bits specified in *expression2*. Left shifts are zero-filled; right shifts are guaranteed to be zero-filled only if *expression1* is unsigned. Both expressions must yield character or integer values. The value returned has the type of *expression1*.

The following operators return the result of logical operations performed on two character or integer operands: the *bitwise AND* operator &, the *bitwise inclusive-OR* operator ¦, and the *bitwise exclusive-OR* operator ^.

The *logical negation* operator ! was mentioned on page 69 and used in several of our example programs. It takes the form

! *expression*

and returns an integer value of zero if *expression* is nonzero, or a value of 1 if *expression* is zero.

C provides a number of assignment operators in addition to the familiar = . In general, they condense assignments of the form *variable* = *variable operator expression*

to the simpler form

*variable operator*= *expression*

For instance, x = x + y becomes x += y.  The complete list of assignment operators is as follows:

$$
\begin{array}{cc}
= & >>= \\
+= & <<= \\
-= & \&= \\
*= & \char94= \\
/= & \char124= \\
\%= &
\end{array}
$$

## Chapters 6 and 11: Control Structures

C programmers can directly alter the flow of control in a function by inserting the statement

    goto *label*;

where *label* is a legal C name followed by a colon that has been inserted in the source code as a destination for the goto:

    label:

It's well known that too-free use of goto's can spoil the structure of a program.  The goto is useful, however, for escaping from deeply nested loops when fatal errors are encountered.

## Chapter 8: Preprocessor

We left out several seldom-used preprocessor commands.  #undef *name* causes *name* to become undefined—that is, to lose the definition it was previously given by #define. This may be important if you're using #ifdef and #ifndef, which take the forms

```
#ifdef name
     .
     .
     .
#endif
```

and

```
#ifndef name
     .
     .
     .
#endif
```

If *name* is (or, with #ifndef, is not) defined, the code between #ifdef (or #ifndef) and #endif is included in the compilation. Otherwise, it's omitted.  You may also write

```
#ifdef name
     .
     .
     .
#else
     .
     .
     .
#endif
```

and likewise for #ifndef. If *name* isn't defined, the code between #else and #endif will be compiled. If it is, the code between #ifdef and #else is included. There's also the arithmetic #if, used this way:

```
#if constant
     .
     .
     .
#endif
```

The code is compiled if *constant* is nonzero.
      The command

```
#line constant
```

simply resets the C compiler's line counter to *constant*.

The command

```
#line constant name
```

resets the current line number of the source code to *constant* and resets the current source file name to *name*.

## Chapter 10: Pointers

Pointers to functions turn up fairly often in C. This is not the place to discuss the how and why, but we should mention the syntax used. This statement declares `fnptr` to be a pointer to an integer function:

```
int (*fnptr)();
```

And this statement sets `fnptr` to point to the function `afunc`, assuming that `afunc` has been properly declared:

```
fnptr = afunc;
```

Note that the function's name, like an array's name, serves as its address. The following statement actually invokes `afunc`, which we assume to take one argument, and returns its value to `x`:

```
x = (*fnptr)(arg);
```

## Chapter 12: Structures

C has no single-bit data type, but as a convenience it provides a way of creating and referencing data values that contain a specified number of bits. Special structure members called *bit fields* do the job. Suppose we're making a longevity study and want to store the following data for each test subject: age, sex, number of surviving parents, number of surviving grandparents. We might base our records on this structure template, which packs the information into four bit fields:

```
struct test_subject
  {
  int sex : 1;
  int parents : 2;
  int grandparents : 3;
  int age : 7;
  };
```

The number to the right of the : tells how many bits to allot for the field. One bit is needed for sex, two for number of surviving parents, and so forth. Bit fields are packed into a single integer; if there are too many bits, they'll spill over into the next int. Once established, a bit field may be referenced like any other member of a structure.

union's borrow the syntax of structures to set aside storage space for variables whose data type may vary. Imagine that we want to declare an array any of whose elements may be a character, an integer, or a pointer to some other array element. We begin by declaring this union template:

```
union mixed_array
  {
  char a_letter;
  int an_integer;
  union mixed_array *a_pointer;
  };
```

Now we can declare the array

```
union mixed_array buffer[BUFSIZE];
```

This tells the compiler to give each element of the array buffer enough space to store the largest of the three types which may go into it—a char, an int, or a pointer to another element. If we know that buffer[n] contains an integer value, we can print it via

```
printf("%d\n", buffer[n].an_integer);
```

If we know it contains a character, we might use

```
printf("%c\n", buffer[n].a_letter);
```

If we know it contains a pointer to an element which contains an integer, we can print the integer with

```
printf("%d\n", buffer[n].a_pointer->an_integer);
```

## Chapter 13: Input/Output and Library Functions

Since your implementation of C may differ in some details from the implementation described here, we won't even try to list all the functions available on our reference compiler. We will just touch briefly on those functions that are most widely used in production C code. For details specific to your installation, refer to your compiler's user manual.

The function `fopen` is used to open files for reading and writing. This is its header:

```
FILE *fopen(fname, type)
char *fname, *type;
```

Programs using `fopen` must include the system file `stdio.h`, which uses `typedef` to define the data type `FILE`. `fname` is a string naming the file to be opened; `type` is one of the following strings (note the double quotes): `"r"` to open a file for reading only; `"w"` to open a file and write from the beginning (so any old contents are lost); `"a"` to open a file and append to it (so old contents are preserved). The value returned by `fopen` is a pointer which should be used in all subsequent references to the file. (The file's name is never referred to again.) A program using `fopen` might contain these lines:

```
#include <stdio.h>
      .
      .
      .
FILE *input_file, *output_file;
      .
      .
      .
input_file = fopen("scores", "r");
output_file = fopen("grades", "w");
```

The file named `scores` is opened for reading and associated with the identifier `input_file`; the file named `grades` is opened for writing and associated with the identifier `output_file`.

`fopen` opens files for *buffered* I/O, a kind of I/O that hides the messiness of reading and writing from the user. Once a file is open, you can access it via functions much like those described in Chapter 13:

`getc`, `putc`, `fgets`, `fprintf`, and `fscanf`. All should be compiled with `stdio.h`.

`getc` and `putc`, like `getchar` and `putchar`, are macros. They may be thought of as functions having these headers:

```
int getc(fid)
FILE *fid;

int putc(c, fid)
char c;
FILE *fid;
```

`fid` is a *file identifier* returned by `fopen`. In terms of our last example, `getc(input_file)` would read the next character from the file named `scores`, while `putc('B', output_file)` would write the character B out to `grades`. When `getc` reaches the end of the file, it returns **EOF**.

`fgets` and `fputs` have these headers:

```
char *fgets(string, size, fid)
char *string;
int size;
FILE *fid;

int fputs(string,fid)
char *string;
FILE *fid;
```

`fgets` reads from a file up to the next newline, or it reads the next `size - 1` characters, whichever comes first. It differs a bit from `gets`—the newline, if any, is retained and followed by a null character, so the string will always be `size` bytes long.

`fprintf` and `fscanf` behave just like `printf` and `scanf`, except of course that they write to and read from files. Here are their headers:

```
fprintf(fid, format_string, arg1, arg2, ... argn)
FILE *fid;
char *format_string;

fscanf(fid, format_string, argptr1, argptr2, ... argptrn)
FILE *fid;
char *format_string;
```

C's file I/O need not be strictly sequential; the function `fseek`
allows you to read from or write to any byte in an `fopen`'d file:

```
#include <stdio.h>

int fseek(fid, offset, mode)
FILE *fid;
long int offset;
int mode;
```

The value `offset` positions your next read or write to `offset`
number of bytes from the file's beginning (if `mode` is 0), from the
file's end (if `mode` is 2), or from the byte you would expect to get
next if you didn't use `fseek` (if `mode` is 1). `offset` may be a
negative number, so you can move back and forth at will through the
file. Here's a sample program that opens the file `test.c` and prints it
backwards at the user's terminal. Note that `fseek` returns 0 unless
you attempt to seek beyond the ends of a file.

```
% cat test.c
#include <stdio.h>

main()
{
   FILE *ptr;

   ptr = fopen("test.c", "r");      /* open for read */
   fseek(ptr, 1L, 2);            /* seek 1 beyond end */
   while (!fseek(ptr, -2L, 1))   /* back up 1 char */
     putchar(getc(ptr));         /* print the char */
}
% cc test.c
% a.out

}
/* rahc eht tnirp */     ;))rtp(cteg(rahctup
/* rahc 1 pu kcab */     ))1 ,L2- ,rpt(keesf!( elihw
/* dne dnoyeb 1 kees */        ;)2 ,L1 ,rtp(keesf
/* daer rof nepo */    ;)"r" ,"c.tset"(nepof = rtp

;rtp* ELIF
{
)(niam

>h.oidts< edulcni#%
```

Note the use of long offset values. $-2L$ is used to back up one character, since each `getc` moves us forward one.

When you're done with a file that was opened with `fopen`, close it with `fclose`:

```
int fclose(fid)
FILE *fid;
```

This tidies up the buffers used by the system. `fclose` returns zero if successful, `EOF` if not.

The functions `open`, `creat`, `read`, `write` and `close` are used for unbuffered I/O. Such operations tend to be very system-dependent and will not be discussed. Refer to your user's manual.

Dynamic memory allocation (i.e., allocation during program execution) is available through the library function `malloc`:

```
char *malloc(size)
unsigned int size;
```

`malloc` returns a pointer to a block of memory large enough to store `size` bytes. When the allocated block is no longer needed, it may be freed by passing the pointer to `free`:

```
free(pointer)
char *pointer;
```

When fewer than `size` bytes of memory are available, `malloc` returns a zero.

# Index

231

## About the Authors

L. HANCOCK, a consultant to Bell Labs on a large data-base system, has worked since 1970 for various firms in the computer industry as a programmer, technical writer, and language instructor. He obtained his B.A. and M.A. in English literature from the University of Miami, and is currently working on completing his requirements for his Ph.D.

M. KRIEGER is a writer and editor specializing in scientific and technical subjects. Formerly a science editor with various publishers and a writer/editor with the publications division of Bell Labs, he is the author of numerous magazine articles and books in both the biological and physical sciences. Interested in computers since 1974, he is co-author of *Structured Microprocessor Programming*. He obtained his B.A. in history from Wayne University.